SMALL WORLDS

ALSO BY ROBERT KLOSE

Adopting Alyosha: A Single Man Finds a Son in Russia

SMALL WORLDS

ADOPTED SONS,

PET PIRANHAS,

AND OTHER MORTAL CONCERNS

ROBERT KLOSE

UNIVERSITY OF MISSOURI PRESS
COLUMBIA AND LONDON

Library of Congress Cataloging-in-Publication Data

Klose, Robert.
  Small worlds : adopted sons, pet piranhas, and other mortal concerns /
Robert Klose.
      p. cm.
  Summary: "Collected essays by Robert Klose, longtime contributing essayist
for the Christian Science Monitor. In a style comparable to that of Garrison
Keillor and Jean Shepherd, Klose shares his experiences raising adoptive sons,
stories of traveling abroad, memories of his childhood, and depictions of life
in his small Maine community"—Provided by publisher.
  ISBN-13: 978-0-8262-1675-5 (pbk. : alk. paper)
  ISBN-10: 0-8262-1675-7 (pbk. : alk. paper)
  I. Title.
  PN4874.K5737A25 2006
  814'.54—dc22   2006014150

Designer: Jennifer Cropp
Typesetter: Crane Composition, Inc.
Printer and binder: The Maple-Vail Manufacturing Group
Typefaces: Minion and Copperplate

Credits appear on page 185.

FOR ALYOSHA AND ANTON

MOST HONORABLE SONS

Contents

A SON FROM RUSSIA

A SON FROM UKRAINE

CLARINETISTRY

NOSTALGIA

TRAVELS

LIVING LANGUAGE

Acknowledgments

I would like to thank Owen Thomas, my longtime editor at *The Christian Science Monitor,* for his keen editorial eye and his unfailing encouragement. This openness to my work continues with his successor, Judy Lowe.

In small proportions we just beauties see,
And in short measures life may perfect be.

Ben Jonson

SMALL WORLDS

LIVING IN MAINE

In Maine it is possible to divide people into two groups: those who chill easily and those who don't chill at all.

I fall into the former category, a significant liability in a place where the first snows frequently arrive in October and the last do not depart until April—six months of virtual winter.

The pursuit of warmth is a prime occupation in Maine. I have never lived in a place with more heating oil companies or more stores that deal in woodstoves. Despite our latitude, even solar energy companies are making a go of it here. I know of a farmer who insulated his entire house with sheep's wool. And in a town north of my home, an ingenious man has invented a furnace that will burn anything, including old boots and Coke bottles. In this corner of the world, cold truly is the mother of invention.

Just before the recent holidays I set out on my annual drive for a good three-dollar wreath for my front door. A few miles outside of Bangor I spotted some for sale by the side of the road. The easel display stood right next to the tiniest house I had ever seen: a peel-paint, clapboard affair, its frame warped and its roof so old that moss was growing among the asphalt shingles. I picked out my wreath, knocked on the door, and in the next moment was confronted by a small, elderly woman bundled in sweaters. I looked past her and saw the one room she lived in, its far corner harboring a bulldog of a woodstove, glowing red in the joints and hissing. "How are you today?" I greeted her. A smile rose on her face. "Keeping warm," she nodded into the collar of her outermost sweater.

I immediately felt a kinship with the wreath lady, realizing that she too was one of the chilled. I paid her the three dollars and left with my treasure.

I have often wondered why people live in cold places. The word *allure* is identified with the north but never with the south. It is as if there is a palpable pull from the boreal reaches of the earth and a seductively benign danger associated with "going north." The very idea connotes risky behavior, a grappling with forces which puts an exclamation point on the act of living. E. Annie Proulx, in her novel *The Shipping News,* said it best when she described her main character as going north to Newfoundland "[because] he needed something to brace against."

For those of us who have consciously chosen to live in the north it is a need, then. A need to be where every winter day is a fresh invigoration and the seasons are written in braille. Where bodies are bundled to the point of immobility, houses are banked against the wind with bags of autumn leaves, and it is not uncommon for someone to retrieve a wind-fallen branch for the moment of warmth it may yield in a woodstove. In the south it is possible to lose track of time, but in the north—never: here the thermometer is read before the morning paper; the sap rises in the sugar maples in February as sure as the snow continues to fall; and the expression "winter solstice" has the sparkle of poetry about it.

What it comes down to is that it is easy to celebrate the north as long as one has a warm place to go. I'm sure Robert Frost had this in mind when he wrote:

> Now close the windows and hush all the fields:
>   If the trees must, let them silently toss;
> No bird is singing now, and if there is,
>   Be it my loss.
>
> It will be long ere the marshes resume,
>   It will be long ere the earliest bird:
> So close the windows and hear not the wind,
>   But see all wind-stirred.

It is the culture of the north that keeps me here, in spite of the cold. And yet I can't help but think of those who might be here because of circumstances beyond their control. In this light, I was recently moved to honor the efforts of a fellow Mainer to stay warm. Brushing the new snow from my woodpile, I put together a tight bundle of kindling. Then I drove a few miles outside of Bangor to the shack where the wreath lady lived. Silently, and leaving only footprints in the snow as a sign of my passing, I laid the bundle at her doorstep and then drove away.

We are all in this together.

It is autumn now in Maine. As if on cue, the days have turned appreciably cooler, the mornings downright cold. The leaves of the silver maples along the river behind my house have reddened along their edges, a preamble to their cascading to earth in swirling droves.

In my neighborhood I hear the sound of axes and chain saws—their rhythms hurried and incessant, as if in apology for being so late at the task of cutting and splitting the firewood which will act as bulwark against the winter that already nips at the heels of fall.

Autumn plainly is the season that most befits Maine, showing her off to maximum effect. The sight of an apple orchard splaying itself out alongside a white clapboard farmhouse, the trees slowly balding yet still holding onto their stark red fruits, is beauty in the extreme. I watch as children scurry among the windfalls while their parents reach for the bright globes of the Cortland, Wealthy, and McIntosh. Soon the cider will begin to flow, and when the sweating jugs finally land on the kitchen table—ambrosia.

Several years ago I had a visit from a dear German friend. Proud, talkative, and unrestrained in celebrating the virtues of his homeland, he spoke of German culture as something so captivating that he could not bear to be away from it for long. I have lived in Germany, and it is true that Germans spell culture with a capital K (for *Kultur*). The country is peppered with museums and monuments; books are venerated as works of art; and every village seems to have its own orchestra (or two).

As I showed him around Maine, we discussed these things, and a comparison was inevitably drawn between our two homes, which are so unlike. Germany is crowded, metropolitan, and hurried. Maine is sparsely populated, rural, and sedate. It has museums, of course, but they are few and far between and are not part of the state's "image." When an orchestra performs, it is truly an event of note. And so I understood how a cultured German might feel forlorn here.

I understood, but I was not prepared for my friend's concluding remark. "Maine has no culture," he declaimed as we sat on the rocks at Schoodic Point. He said this during a storm surge, his pronouncement embedded in the crashing of waves and the squawking of gulls. I thought for a moment, and then I smiled.

Plainly, I had not done a very good job of acculturating him to life in the north country. For a moment I considered identifying our museums, theaters, and small cities, but such a head-on assault would have failed miserably: Bangor is no Berlin. The culture of Maine is not one of bricks and mortar. Rather, it is a product of its natural landscape as well as the habits, traditions, and attitudes of a relatively small population of hearty souls who live in a cold place which juts into the North Atlantic like a balled fist.

What is Maine culture to me? In summer it is a Downeast beach that I can have all to myself, an opportunity for natural peace, an ever-diminishing commodity in an increasingly hectic world. In July it is the visit to a "pick-your-own" strawberry farm, where and I crawl among the rows, picking and eating, the knees of my jeans red and sopping with the juice of the berries I have crushed underneath.

In spring the rivers swell with cashiered snow—the bounty rushing audibly to the sea. Behind my very house the Penobscot sluices along, choked with the ice which sings like a cacophony of broken glass that shimmers blue in the sunlight. I stand on the bank and observe the scene, shoulder to shoulder with neighbors, all of us clinging to a moment which will soon be gone.

Winters are contradances in Grange halls, bean suppers in churches, cross-country skiing under the snow-laden boughs of white pines, home fires kindled with apple branches, and children ice-skating until the sun goes down. It is an opportunity to generally move more slowly, to assess the summer that's gone by and feel forward, with hope, for the spring to come.

And now it is autumn, and my heart quickens with the pulse of the land. There is a sense of urgency as school gets a foothold, sunlight becomes a rare commodity, and there are reports of snow in the mountains. Some folks behave as if a trace of summer still lingers—I see them in short sleeves, mowing lawns or sitting quietly on park benches, reading books and sipping orange juice. But this is nostalgia for that which is gone and will not return for a very long while. Before long they will understand and accept this, too, and will join the mass of Mainers in slipping neatly—and inevitably—into winter, when pretense will no longer be possible.

I tell these things to my German friend as we sit on the rocks at Schoodic Point. He smiles and nods, and I know he is only moderately receptive to my words. Before long the wind becomes stronger and colder.

We zip up our collars and huddle off to the car, where the argument about culture continues all the way back to Bangor.

After he had returned to Germany I received a letter from him. He told me that on his drive back to Logan Airport in Boston he passed a Maine farmhouse that had a sign out front: *This is our spring for your use. Enjoy.*

He remarked that it was the best water he had ever tasted and that he couldn't believe the people in that farmhouse were willing to share it for free. "I miss Maine," he wrote in closing.

I now realize that I had made little headway by extolling Maine's virtues to my German friend. I hadn't considered that my culture was perfectly capable of speaking for itself, in a softer voice—the quiet percolation of a farmhouse spring.

RIVER PUMPKINS

The other day there were pumpkins bobbing in the river behind my house.

Pumpkins in the Penobscot!

I later learned that they had fallen from a truck as it rumbled over the small bridge just upstream.

I discovered them early in the morning. I had gone out to the riverbank for a few quiet moments before leaving for work. I watched as the mist slowly lifted from the water, revealing the orange globes bumping up against a nearshore bar like aquatic mammals coming in to feed. I watched them for quite a while, as if there were something more they could possibly show me. But I decided the mere fact of pumpkins in the river was remarkable enough, and I headed off to the university.

Still, I couldn't get them off my mind. As I stood at the blackboard, lecturing on natural selection, my thoughts were constantly drifting back to the river pumpkins. I came precariously close to losing my thread of thought, but when one is teaching biology to freshman non-majors, control is everything, and so I persisted in describing how animals and plants are physically and behaviorally adapted to their environments. And then my mind drifted again. Here I was describing why the snowshoe rabbit's fur turns white in a winter landscape, and I had pumpkins bobbing in the river behind my house. I felt the strongest need to get back to them. To see what they were up to. I drove home with a special—and unprofessional—urgency at the end of the work-day. Relief came only when I went down to the river and saw the pumpkins. Safe and sound. Only they had increased from the original eight or so to an even dozen as a nearshore eddy herded them up against the bar.

As I turned to go in I was greeted by the little boy next door, who had come for a visit. Actually, seven-year-old Russell had moped over for a visit. I had never seen him so sad. The problem, as he told it, was that "all the other kids" had jack-o-lanterns—except for him. His mother wouldn't let him have one. "She said they have bugs and things," he lamented. Bugs!

A child's dreams are often about the impossible—to fly like Super-man, to knock down a brick wall, to travel to another world—but some-times they are small and manageable and the solution is, like a rare alignment of planets, foreordained. I suddenly knew what I had to do. "Russell," I said, bending low, "your friends have field pumpkins. Any-one can have a field pumpkin." I added that I could get him something far more special.

Russell screwed up his face and cocked his head to the side. "What?"

I whispered into his ear, "A river pumpkin."

Russell's eyes flashed. "A river pumpkin?" he echoed.

"Yes," I assured him. "Every year, up north in Millinocket, the big field pumpkins break from their vines and roll into the river, where they be-come river pumpkins. Then they float all the way down here so little boys and girls can have them for Halloween."

Russell's eyes grew as big and bright as moons. "Really?" he begged.

"Yes," I said. "Just look." I pointed toward the river, and Russell, seeing the pumpkins, was absolutely transported. "Let's go," I said.

Gathering life jackets and paddles, we clambered into my canoe and set out over the cool, dark, leaf-littered water. Russell perched over the bow like a figurehead. Within a couple of minutes the canoe was nosing in among the pumpkins. As they bumped up against the sides of the boat Russell reached down and grabbed hold of one a little larger than a basketball. I steadied the canoe as he wrestled it over the gunnel.

Like the whalers of old Boston we sailed home with our bounty. I watched as Russell, now grinning from ear to ear, wrapped his arms around the pumpkin and stumbled out of the canoe and up the riverbank. I continued to watch, following at a distance, as he did a bandy-legged two-step up his front walk, struggling with his load. His mother came out of the house, hands on her hips, obviously building up steam for a reprimand. "Where did you get that?" she demanded. "I told you you couldn't have a pumpkin."

Russell hefted his load before his mother's eyes. "But Mom," he pleaded, his voice already quivering. "You said I couldn't have a *field* pumpkin. This is a river pumpkin."

"A what?"

"A river pumpkin," repeated Russell. And then he recited, "Every year up in Millinocket the field pumpkins roll into the river and become river pumpkins. Then they come down here for boys and girls to take. Honest."

The part about the migratory habits of pumpkins was too much for his mother, and I could see her ire rising. As for me, I knew that there were times when moral support just wasn't enough. A legend must be related by one person and then sworn to by another. I came around the corner of the house and up behind Russell. "Mighty fine river pumpkin you got there, Russ."

The mother's eyebrows took flight. "River pumpkin? You mean . . . ?"

"I have five myself," I said. "Easier to carve. Beats a field pumpkin hands down. And no bugs!" And then, "You do know the story of the river pumpkins, don't you? Well, every year, up in Millinocket . . ."

That night there was a jack-o-lantern flaring in the front window of Russell's home. And it had stories to tell.

A WARM WELCOME FOR A TARDY WINTER

This year, winter in Maine got off to a tepid start. When one lives in a cold place, and it doesn't behave like a cold place, strange things happen.

It hit fifty degrees shortly before Christmas. Warm stuff for a Maine December. Daisies were in bloom, ladybugs were crawling along the windowsills, lake water was rippling, and, as I walked through the woods, a great blue heron rose from the reeds bordering a small pond. The herons are usually gone by November, but this one slowly lifted itself on expansive wings, headed south, and then, as if perplexed, turned north.

There was no snow for quite a while, which meant there was no better reason for Mainers to speak of snow. Incessantly. Snow is considered a bother by most people, but Mainers actually anticipate the stuff. Someone once told me that's because the people here want something to complain about, but I think that's terribly cynical. Snow is visible confirmation that we do, indeed, live in Maine—up here in the northeast corner of the country, at the end of the line, not on the way to anyplace, which is the way most folks seem to like it.

But the warmth and lack of snow make people behave in peculiar ways. My son, for example. He received a snowboard as an early Christmas gift. Complete with boots and bindings. Outside it was dry and barren as a bone, but that didn't keep Alyosha from strapping on the board and shunting himself back and forth over the living room carpet.

I've heard of such a thing in parakeets. It's called "vacuum behavior." A parakeet has such a strong urge to fly that, when confined to its cage for more than a couple of days, it periodically takes frantic and protracted wing. Not because it has anywhere to go, or because there's any hope of escape, but because the impulse to fly is overwhelming. It builds up. Thus it was with Alyosha and his snowboard. The next morning, when I went to wake him, I found him in bed with the thing still strapped to his feet.

Vacuum behavior.

The unusual weather affected others as well. One morning I ran into a friend who had a kayak lashed to the roof of her car. "A kayak?" I remarked.

She grew stern. "Sure," she said. "Why not? I mean, do you really think it's going to snow this year?"

I understood immediately. She was frustrated with winter for not being itself. By breaking out her kayak she was performing an incantation of sorts, hoping to move the powers that be to get back on track, become their old selves, hold forth with cold, snow, and ice.

I sympathized with all of these things—the daisies, the great blue heron, my son, and the lady with the kayak. I felt something too. I sensed myself perched ripe for the advent of a true winter, not quite imploring it to arrive but anticipating it every time I walked outside. I would look up at the sky and squint at the fixed, gray cloud cover, ready at any moment to blink my lids shut in case the flakes should start to come down in earnest.

If the truth be told, warmth is a bad thing for winter. Because both people and the land depend on the cold for so many things. It puts animals and plants to rest so that they can make a decent go of it in the spring. It fills the high places with ice and snow so the rivers can perform their cleansing act when the thaw comes. It makes the pines look stately and beauteous against the stark, bare maples and poplars.

For me, the cold's most precious virtue is that it slows things down: waterways all but cease their flow; snowy roads signal caution; community suppers in church and Grange halls bring people together for friendly evenings; and woodstoves dictate a rhythm of wood-gathering and -burning which paces us through the long, dark months.

If not for the cold, spring would not be greeted as something spectacular or as a reward for Mainers' showing they were able to "take the winter" yet again and come out somehow the better for it.

I tried to explain some of these observations to my son, but he is thirteen and has learned the adolescent trick of displaying higher intelligence by looking at me as if I come from a primitive, less sophisticated culture. I think, though, that he would like my thoughts about learning to love the cold. He is, after all, in possession of a brand-new snowboard, and since the winter's warm preamble, temperatures have dropped and heavy snows have fallen.

Both Alyosha and I will now enjoy this appropriately cold season, each in his own way. My carpet, too, if it could speak, would be grateful.

WHY I PREFER AN AX TO A SPLITTER

The other day I was out in the backyard, doing my Paul Bunyan routine as I swung my ax over my shoulder and came down hard and clean against the wood I had hauled from the Penobscot River and then hand-sawed. The wood was dry and well seasoned; if I was right on the mark, I could cleave it with a single swift chop.

It was hovering just above zero outside—a bracing morning in central Maine. I chopped apace and my woodpile grew. It wasn't long before a passerby called out from the road: "Get a splitter!"

It was a good-natured jab, and my critic waved as he hurried on his way. On such a frigid morning, with hoarfrost illuminating the roof shingles, I was flattered that he had chosen to stop at all, for interrupting one's stride even for a moment allows the cold to seep in. It's always best to keep moving.

Of course, there are moments when I realize that a gas-powered wood splitter would be a boon to my efficiency and would let me get out of the cold that much sooner. But I chop wood with an ax for a variety of reasons. One is the slow, waxing burn I kindle in my muscles as I work away. After a few minutes of wielding the ax, I am pushing the cold back, like a wave, overcoming it with my own burgeoning warmth. I like being able to do this, to say, in effect, yes, it is cold outside, but what of it?

Then there is the pure artistry of it. A well-swung ax is poetry in motion. I love the heft of the tool, the silence with which it moves down through the air, and the final "chock!" as a piece of timber is hewn and the two halves fly off in opposite directions, affording me whiffs of the resinous heartwood.

But the most compelling reason for my choice of tools is the feel of the ax handle. When I bought my hundred-year-old house, I found the ax in a corner of the woodshed. Its handle is polished hickory, rendered smooth by the hands of who knows how many before me, who have stood where I stand, hefting and chopping, generation upon generation.

An ax handle, or helve, is a thing of beauty, having long ago reached design perfection. Picture the letter "S." Now stretch it out and take most of the curve out of the upper and lower loops. What you're left with is exactly the right shape for the job at hand, a sort of lever with the human arm as its fulcrum. It is this shape that allows for the right grip, the right velocity, the right angle, the right everything. Wielding an ax would be a very different experience if the handle were straight; it would be akin to swinging a bat. But an ax handle's mildly sinusoidal aspect lends one the feeling of springing a trap.

Can one really wax poetic about such things? Of course. It's already been done by Robert Frost in "The Ax-Helve," in which his main character despairs over having purchased an ax showing poor workmanship:

> "Made on machine," he said, plowing the grain
> With a thick thumbnail to show how it ran
> Across the handle's long-drawn serpentine,

Like the two strokes across a dollar sign.
"You give her one good crack, she's snap raght off."

And the poet Gary Snyder wrote a piece titled, of all things, "Axe Handles," in which he sees himself as an ax, a model for his son, whose spirit he describes as an ax handle still taking form:

I am an axe
And my son a handle, soon
To be shaping again, model
And tool, craft of culture,
How we go on.

My ax has enabled me to learn to love the winter—absolutely essential if one intends to come to peace with living in such a cold and climatically unpredictable place as Maine. I have to admit that there have been moments when I have gone outside in a blizzard as a result of my not having cut enough wood. As the gales burn my face, I chop. As the snow sneaks in under my collar, I chop. At such moments I come close to regretting the ax and wishing for the splitter. But in everything lost there is something gained.

At this writing I am still holding the hickory tight, steady as she goes.

THE RIVER AND I AWAKEN

Last night the river spoke. It was enough to wake me from sleep: the brief thud, echoing ever so slightly in the still-bare woods. The first collapse of ice. The river flexing its muscles as it stirred from winter sleep.

This preparatory, tentative breakup of the Penobscot River filled me with the first real sense that spring was under way. Have the days really been warm enough to melt the eighteen-inch-thick ice? I could still clearly recall the river's November voice, when the ice first started to form. As the water expanded and hardened, it felt inland a ways, embracing the thick, peeling trunks of the silver maples which line the river's banks. And then, as I stood watching and listening, the river paused and settled, and the ice fractured, sounding like cracks of gunfire. Then it began again, the thickening, the rising, the spreading out over the floodplain, the settling. By December it was done, and snow lay like a blanket on that which had finally nodded off.

This morning I went outside at first light to see how far things had come since the river cleared its throat last night. There it was, down the middle of the frozen sheet, all along its length: the ice had collapsed, and a shallow pool of frigid water had seeped up into the depression. Soon it will begin to flow. We are at the point of no return then.

When I went into town for groceries I took time out at a café. While sitting down to tea I overheard a woman speaking animatedly about, of all things, the stretch of river where she lived. "I think of moving sometimes," she told her partner in conversation, "but . . . well, once you've lived on a river, there really are no other options."

Exactly. That was exactly it. I had to interrupt her. Affirm her in her commitment to river life. "Did you hear it?" I asked her. "The ice breaking during the night?"

Not yet. She lived a few miles to the north of me, where the ice was even thicker. "Don't worry," I told her. "Any day now. Any moment."

She left the café, quivering with anticipation.

We are of a kind, we river dwellers. Our homes are bounded by land on three sides, but on the fourth is our connection to the ocean. The river, then, is actually my window on the world. I must have it, or I would feel landlocked. A pond or lake just can't compare. I once got into this debate with a friend of mine who owns a cabin on a Maine lake. She described it as somehow superior to rivers because her lake is idyllic, placid, glasslike, respectful of borders.

Little did she know that she was making my point for me. Rivers are different from other freshwater bodies exactly because they are not placid or glasslike, nor prone to staying put. Rivers are alive. Even John Masefield, a former poet laureate of England, took time out from writing saltwater ballads to pay tribute to the enduring quality of rivers:

> All other waters have their time of peace,
> Calm, or the turn of tide or summer drought;
> But on these bars the tumults never cease

I suppose I have a real sense that folks who live on ponds or lakes are playing it safe, not taking life by the horns. They don't enjoy that heightened sense of mortality when the river speaks in spring. Perhaps this is why my neighbors perform annual river walks, approaching the half-melted bank, pushing against a remnant of ice with the toe of a boot, wondering how far the water might rise, how close they can come to something so whimsical in its moods. But no matter how fierce and threatening the spring runoff, no matter how long and hard and dreary the winter has been, by May they will dismiss all thoughts of moving to Florida and wonder how they will ever get any work done at all, so occupied are they with resting their eyes upon the river.

It is April now. The channel in the center of the river has widened, and the water is noodling its way through, gurgling just loud enough to be heard. Soon plates of ice will peel away from the banks, spinning and bobbing south, like seagoing mammals at play. Then the river will swell. Once it has opened wide there will be a massive wash of ice from the north, the chunks blue and sparkling, nudging against each other, tinkling like crushed glass. Finally, it will be done, the great catharsis. The river will feel for its natural borders again, settle in, and from day to day will be different. Rising in times of rain, receding in drought. Canoes and kayaks will color its surface. On the rare day when it disguises itself as a lake, the girl down the road will float off in her inner tube, reading a novel under the sun and dreaming of love. My own boy will wander its muddy banks, earnestly plodding in search of frogs.

As for me, on a bad day I will wonder if another house, another neighborhood, another state are in order. And who knows what the future will bring? For now, though, I wrest myself from the lure of errant thought. For the moment, at least, I belong to the river as much as it belongs to me.

MAINE'S LITERATURE OF SWAP OR SELL

Maine is a paradise for those interested in odds and ends, bric-a-brac, antiques, and assorted junk. As such, there exists up here a sort of clearinghouse for secondhand items in the form of a weekly publication called *Uncle Henry's*, a self-described "Swap or Sell It Guide" where you can buy, sell, or trade almost anything imaginable.

Published on newsprint, *Uncle Henry's* has the feel of a cheap novel, its ink still sweet when it comes off the presses on Thursday afternoons. It can be found in any convenience store, stacked neatly next to the cash register, where people actually stand around waiting for it to be delivered. It is avidly devoured by the masses, from truck drivers to attorneys, fishermen to physicians, making its weekly appearance one of the most democratic events in the state.

But *Uncle Henry's* is more than a weekly shopper. It is literature. Anyone who's ever read it can tell you this. Although its microscopic ads are divided up into mundane categories such as autos, stoves, building materials, and musical instruments, most folks I know aren't looking for a specific item. They read it cover to cover, the way they would a riveting book.

I have collected some of the more colorful ads over the years, to give an idea of the flavor of this wonderful periodical. Consider this one, wedged magnificently between a request for old clocks and one for the rear seat of a '79 Ford pickup: *Wanted: fruit trees, dead or alive.* It's an attention-grabber and makes one ponder the motives of the writer, the way any good novel would.

The examples of good and entertaining writing are legion. A few years back, when I was looking for a secondhand clarinet for my son, I came across the following, from a clearly frustrated parent: *Clarinet For Sale. Cheap. (Now he wants the trumpet!).* And consider this one for a reliable polly: *Parrot. Free to a good home. I let him fly outside and he always comes back (so far).*

The most popular category is "Free for the Taking." Need a piano? You'll find one here, as touted by one inconvenienced soul: *Piano. Take it. It's in my way.* Or this recurring ad for garden enthusiasts: *Free Manure! All you want. (I'll help you load it!).*

When one succeeds in securing an item that hasn't already been sold (the competition is keen), the people one meets frequently add interest to the transaction. Just last year I found a bargain in a woodstove and drove deep into Maine's hill country to pick it up. I arrived at a magnificent cedar home the retired owner had built with his own hands. Admiring his work, I asked if he was an architect or contractor. He told me he had worked for NASA as an aerospace engineer but was now a certified hypnotist. The conversation took wing from there, and when we were done I came away with a six-hundred-dollar woodstove for a song, and a good story to boot.

Although *Uncle Henry's* contains generally good, practical Yankee stuff like bricks, tires, screw augers, and fishing reels, the esoteric sometimes makes an appearance, addressing more Bohemian sensibilities. This was the case a couple of years back, when an ad appeared for the mummy of an Egyptian cleric. The asking price was $40,000. I don't know if any thrifty, utilitarian Mainer answered the ad, but I was impressed with the author's closing gloss, which was straight out of the history books: *Will no one rid me of this meddlesome priest? (Call after 6 P.M.)*.

The upshot of all this is that *Uncle Henry's* represents some of the best writing in the state of Maine and should be wedged neatly between Longfellow and E. B. White. I once visited a home where hundreds of the brightly colored volumes lined a shelf, afforded a prominence befitting the *Encyclopedia Britannica*. It seemed perfectly appropriate, and before I knew it I was deep into my reading, wondering how I would ever get through all of them before being asked to leave.

Now that the warm weather has arrived, *Uncle Henry's* has swelled to robust proportions with the harvests of spring-cleaned barns and attics. As I page through it my eye is seized by an ad for, of all things, a trolley jack. Yes, I need one of those, don't I? For ten dollars it's a steal, and once I lug the thing home I'm sure I'll find a use for it. If not, I can always post it for sale again.

It's a wonderful thing to live in a place where nothing ever goes to waste.

COMPASSION THAWS MAINE'S GREAT FREEZE

Yesterday diamonds fell from a clear blue sky.

That was my impression as I stood by my living room window, watching the immense silver maple in my front yard. For four days running, Maine had endured a winter storm the likes of which did not exist in modern memory. It left power lines, eaves, and especially the trees jacketed in ice. Then came yesterday's respite: the clouds cleared, and the sun baked the ice free of the branches. It fell for hours with an incessant clatter that had people scurrying through the streets with their hands covering their heads.

Maine is, by nature, a civil place to live. But this civility was put to the test when the storm downed power lines and 400,000 households were suddenly without electricity, which meant, most frighteningly, that most were without heat as well.

In the north country warmth is everything. It is perhaps the central dogma of life here, the one shared understanding: being cold is unacceptable. When the greater part of an entire state goes dark and cold, people's true natures come out in spades. This is because calamity is the great leveler: poor and rich, young and old, strong and weak—all are suddenly in the same boat, taking steps to provide for comfort as well as dignity.

Thus began a poignant outpouring of mutual concern. Radio stations became extended, battery-powered town halls, providing a special warmth of their own as people called in with questions, pleas, advice, and offers of material and emotional support.

My young son and I found it necessary to abandon all of our house except for its humblest corner: the mudroom. This unadorned space had always served as a general depository for tools, cross-country skis, muddy boots, and old newspapers. Its heart was a vintage Sears cast-iron woodstove, which would become our pilot light in a landscape which seemed, to a great extent, forsaken. And so, dragging a mattress down from an upstairs room, Alyosha and I fired up the woodstove, turned on the radio, and hunkered down for the duration.

Even as we endured the long days, a certain human grandeur grew out of the protracted ordeal. Stripped of all but the most elementary technology, the world becomes a very small place indeed. There were many compelling moments when one person's experience resonated for everybody.

Listening to the radio in our mudroom redoubt at night, I realized that people harbor a compelling need to be kind. A woman from some remote corner of the state called with a plea for lamp oil. The next caller not only offered an ample supply, but was willing to deliver it as well. Someone else needed to know how to start a fire without matches. An engineer called in with a recipe for a battery-and-steel-wool gadget guaranteed to do the trick. A young mother called to say that the cold was becoming too much for her and her children. An elderly woman immediately responded and invited the family to her home, and then, after a moment's pause, added, "And anyone else who needs to can come too!"

There were moments of lighter drama as well, such as the boy who desperately needed to know how to keep his pet iguana warm. The rapid response from the next caller: "Put it under your shirt."

The radio station that mediated all of this citizen interaction was called, appropriately, "The Voice of Maine." As its power waned day by day, it went to heroic lengths to keep transmitting. Eventually it had to turn to a propane-fired generator on Passadumkeag Mountain. A lone Samaritan on a snowmobile traveled up the mountain through the dead of night to deliver the gas cylinders.

My son and I took great heart in the continuous broadcast, for if there is one thing more terrible than the cold, it is the fear of being alone in that cold. I thought about this as we lay in the dark next to the steadily pulsing woodstove. Only when I was sure Alyosha's sleep was profound did I venture out to the woodpile to gather more fuel. Slipping across the ice and snow, I was compelled to linger and gaze up at a sky of unbroken clouds. Not a star to be seen. But when I looked across the road, I saw the flickering of solitary candles in the windows of otherwise dark homes. The stars had come to earth, then, and their message was, "We're still here, still making the best of it." Then, my arms full of wood, I hurried back to my son, who had not stirred in my absence.

A time of crisis is a true animator of generosity. One evening, Alyosha and I drove to the house of some friends in the next town. They had already taken in two families, and a third for supper seemed only to heighten the joy they felt in sharing what they had. Each room was appointed with candles, the children were playing card games in the living room, and a shrimp stir-fry sizzled on the woodstove. As we sat down to eat by candlelight, I realized that this scene was being repeated all over the state—a thanksgiving born of necessity.

When Alyosha and I returned home that night the first thing I noticed was that the woodstove had ceased to sputter. I laid my hand on its surface and found it had cooled, having yielded its labor to the now-humming furnace. We had power again. I quickly called the friends we had just left. They were still making due with candles, wood, and blankets.

Before long their electrical power would begin to flow, too, but for the moment I felt cheated. I envied them their community. And then I looked into the living room and saw my son perched in front of the TV, staring at the flickering image. The good old days had roared back upon us with the flip of a switch.

I know I should have rejoiced in my son's return to the affirming normalcy of routine, but it wasn't that easy: all I could think of was that solitary snowmobiler ascending Passadumkeag Mountain with his precious cargo. And so, in tribute to that courageous soul, I went out to the mudroom, stoked the woodstove, and began to read a book by candle-light. I wanted to hang on just a bit longer, before the reanimation of time and technology reclaimed me too.

SMALL STORES HOLD TREASURES THAT MONEY CAN'T BUY

Recently, my small Maine town achieved a victory. Faced with the prospect of a pharmacy chain tearing down a historical building in the village center to put in a so-called superstore, we neighbors confronted the developers themselves at a town meeting and convinced them to abandon the project.

I think that all of us were unprepared for triumph. After all, the chain was promising so much: a drive-through, long hours, and a mind-boggling variety of goods. In an age when surfaces are seductive and in-dividuals feel powerless in the face of industrial wealth, the impassioned voices of locals arguing for the conservation of their small-town atmos-phere and the existing main street pharmacy carried a note of poig-nancy as well as urgency. In short, we knew what we were fighting against, but we also knew what we were fighting *for*. The image that most compels me concerns one of the first experiences I had when I ar-rived in Maine fifteen years ago.

Fresh out of the navy, I was coming to Maine on my motorcycle (ah, yes, I had a motorcycle once . . .). After crossing the Piscataqua River Bridge from New Hampshire, I connected with a rural inland road. I soon needed to gas up, so I pulled into a small, isolated general store. But it was closed. However, there was a hand-lettered sign on one of the two gas pumps: *Owners away. Pump gas and put money in can.*

Put money in can? What can? And there, on the other side of the pump, was a coffee can half-filled with bills. Having been born and raised in New Jersey, I thought this was some kind of joke. But pump I did, and pay I did—happily so. As I drove away, I kept looking over my shoulder, expecting someone to leap out of the woods, grab the cash, and run off.

But that never happened.

In time I learned that in Maine such things are not unusual. The town I settled in also had a store which was one of the wonders of the mercantile world. Laverdiere's was called a pharmacy, but pharmaceuticals were the least of its offerings. Toys, food, greeting cards, fishing tackle, hunting licenses, bug dope . . . I even remember walking down an aisle one day and accidentally knocking a pair of snowshoes from the shelf. And overhead, suspended by wires, was a fully inflated rubber boat, paper streamers taped to its stern and flapping in the gust of an electric fan to indicate sleekness. I would use any excuse to enter this store, if only to behold it all. And if I did buy something and was lacking a few pennies, the owner waved me off and told me not to worry about it.

The thing is, one goes into small, family-owned stores for more than a purchase. Whether it's the hardware store that still sharpens saws on the premises, or the grocery that you can actually walk to, or the general store where they hold a copy of the morning paper for you, the goal is not to simply get there, but to contrive a reason for lingering. In small stores people move more slowly, and they listen in on the conversations of others. Not long ago I was in a local café and stood patiently behind an older man who was buying two bottles of wine. The young woman at the cash register asked him if he wanted them in separate bags. "Oh, no," he protested with a note of horror. "If you do that, how will I hear the bottles chime?"

That utterance moved me more deeply than the most heartfelt speech of any politico. When, I asked myself, was I ever in a large supermarket where the chiming of its bottles was an issue?

Recently, the city of Bangor tore down a perfectly functional neighborhood to make room for a state-of-the-art giant supermarket that opened just last week. Fifty-six thousand square feet! Besides the food, it contains a bank, a pharmacy, and a photo center. Thousands of people flocked to the store as if it had just done a heroic deed and needed to be congratulated. But my heart was heavy. It seemed to offer anticommunity, reasons to get in and get out as quickly as possible: overwhelming crowds, long checkout lines, blaring rock-and-roll, no opportunity to get to know anybody. And what chance did I have in that pandemonium of hearing something so subtle as the chiming of wine bottles?

While tremendous numbers of people patronize these monster stores in pursuit of lower prices, there seem to be just enough of the rest of us to keep a pilot light going for the smaller, family-owned shops. Prices might be a bit higher on average, due to smaller sales volumes, but we live with the people who own these stores, and we thrive on their commitment to the communities they share with us. Their businesses are intimate corners in a landscape which malls and megastores have made too big for the human activities of conversation, fellowship, and benign eavesdropping (those wine bottles!).

I finally did drive to our new giant supermarket yesterday—out of sheer curiosity. The store's spokesman had told reporters on opening day that there were thirty thousand items on the shelves. Despite these riches I felt no compulsion to linger, for there was no idle chatter, no allowance made for missing pennies, and alas, no snowshoes.

SPRING, AND ALREADY APPLES

The first day of spring notwithstanding, it continued to snow up here in central Maine. The weather forecasters on radio and television mentioned the fact of spring, but with a hint of apology in their voices, conveying a sense that they had failed to deliver the correct season on the appointed date.

But the official first day of the new season grants me a right—which did not exist as recently as Groundhog Day—to think in terms of spring and to begin to move as if I will soon be doing great things outdoors, under a brilliant sky, caressed by warmer and more affirming winds, my fingers sunk in the steadily warming earth.

First and foremost I think of apples. They mean a great deal in the north country, because they are one of the few tree fruits that will actually make a respectable go of it in Maine. Plums are said to offer some competition, but I would hesitate to buy a diminutive, rather dessicated Maine plum if given a choice between it and a succulent import. Pears can face the winter here, but the fruit is scrawny, as if all of the tree's reserves have been spent on sheer survival during the coldest months. Some years back a new variety of peach was developed in New Hampshire—the "Reliance"—said to be able to withstand temperatures of twenty below. I bought one, planted it, watched it blossom the very first spring, and then commemorated its passing a year later, after a winter that had seen a temperature of twenty-*one* below.

Apple trees are special because they have, like the poodle, become dependent on human ministrations. An untended apple tree cries for attention by going every which way in the joints and throwing its branches around itself, as if to garner the embrace it lacks from human caretakers. But when they are properly pruned and fertilized and protected from insect pests and fungus, they become sculptures of profound beauty, each variety with its own personality. The Cortland in my backyard, with its dark, shiny bark and symmetrical form has caught the eye of more than one passerby, including a driver who stopped and called me over to his car. "Is that a Cortland?" he asked. When I nodded assent his eyes sparkled. "That is one beautiful tree," he said, lingering a moment before driving on.

The allure of apple trees lies not only in their hardiness and growing form, but in the sheer number of varieties and their appealing nomenclature. Before the fruit became homogenized on supermarket shelves in the form of the Red Delicious ("Cardboard!" scoffs my septuagenarian neighbor Earl), there was a stunning number of different apples available to Americans. Just look at these names: Cox's Orange Pippin, Wolf River, Esopus Spitzenburg, Northern Spy, Oxford, Wealthy, Westfield Seek-No-Further. Each has its own coloration, taste, texture, and keeping qualities. Although they have disappeared from supermarket shelves, they can still be found at roadside stands and farmers' markets, cultivated by people dedicated to their persistence in the gene pool.

In my own town there is a man who raises these "antique" varieties as an avocation. He is a biochemist, and I have seen him at professional meetings, discussing this or that chemical reaction, when suddenly someone asks him about his orchard. Like a ship drawn into a whirlpool, he yields to the inevitable. "Now you've done it," he says, "you've got me going on those apples." From that moment on, the talk never returns to molecules. He cannot help it. He is in love.

We have here in Maine a family that raises fruit trees specifically for our northern climate. Every spring they hold a sale, and folks come from all over the state and beyond to purchase the cultivars. Some come just to admire them. About ten years ago I went to the Fulford family to buy my first apple tree. When I got there, on the second day of the sale, it seemed that all of the trees were gone. I asked the youngest Fulford, Mark, a milk-faced twenty year old, if there was any hope. He thought for a moment and then escorted me to a mere whip with two thin side branches stretched out like waiting arms. "A Cortland," he said in the abbreviated Fulford manner. "Very hardy. Five dollars."

I decided to purchase the tree, but when I moved to take it, Mark seemed reluctant to let go. "These trees," he said wistfully, running his hand up and down the smooth, russet-colored skin and going over it with his eyes. "You know, I just got married, but on my honeymoon all I could think about was these apple trees."

I hesitated for a moment, giving Mark time to accept that I was worthy of the purchase and would take good care of his Cortland. I understood his concern, having read Frost's words about the perils that can befall apple trees:

> *This saying good-by on the edge of the dark*
> *And the cold to an orchard so young in the bark*
> *Reminds me of all that can happen to harm*
> *An orchard away at the end of the farm*

Mark finally released the prize, and today it grows in a sunny spot in my backyard, overlooking the Penobscot River. It is still a young thing, but in the spring it blossoms mightily, in the summer its branches droop with their loads of purple-red fruit, and in autumn it drums the earth with its windfalls.

But enough of spring, summer, and fall. It is late March, and this is Maine, and the Cortland stands snow-laden, which means that I have everything to look forward to.

PEDAGOGY

I am worried about my students. You see, I teach college biology, and from my vantage point in the classroom, I see gaps in what my students know that cannot be filled with huge helpings of facts. They are learning theories, the products of science, but they don't understand the way scientists think.

To me, scientists are among the most interesting people on earth. They are incorrigibly curious and energetic, so much so that their energies spill over into nonscientific pursuits. They not only peek into the contents of living cells, but they play the cello and struggle with translations of Old High German poetry as well. These associated activities aren't tangential; rather, they are expressions of the scientists' need to know "everything."

This is the scientific profession's unspoken goal. In medicine, it is the desire to eradicate all illness. For the physical scientist, it is nothing less than the wish to understand the anatomy of the universe entire. Yet somehow these ambitions are augmented by seemingly incongruous interests like playing Bach and Benny Goodman. This is what makes science an exuberant enterprise. The late science historian Jacob Bronowski makes this point clear in his book *The Origins of Knowledge and Imagination*. Although Albert Einstein played the violin—"execrably" he says—he played it not as a diversion, but as one manifestation of his whole personality.

Although today's scientists also dabble in the arts, there is a pervasive tendency to teach science in a sterile manner, as if other disciplines did not exist. Last semester I introduced a lesson on skeletal anatomy by reading Robert Frost's "The Witch of Coös" aloud to my class. This is a poem about a set of bones that goes for a walk one winter night through a New Hampshire farmhouse, "when the bed might just as well be ice and the clothes snow." My students seemed to enjoy it, and I was not only grateful for their attention but vindicated when a few of them perceived what for our needs was the simple moral of the poem—that bone is alive.

As it turned out, some students had never heard of Frost. Nor of Walt Whitman, Emily Dickinson, or Henry David Thoreau. Does literature belong in the science classroom? Of course. We should not forget that a major reason Charles Darwin's ideas elicited such fire, pro and con, was that his detailed observations were clearly presented in language that in many instances rose to the level of poetry. What worries me about my students is that they don't read the broad range of books that would expand their knowledge of the world around them. For example, they study math but are so intent on mastering equations and formulas that they never grasp the bigger picture—that the world of geometry is a fixed one while calculus, by contrast, was developed to describe the nonlinear motion of objects such as the planets. Unfortunately, science education also fragments related areas of learning, the inference being that they have no bearing on one another.

But to know the world—and the universe—demands more. It requires an awareness of science as a discipline with connections to literature—even to the simplest protocols of grammar. In a profession that stakes its integrity upon the exactness of its mathematical calculations, students must know that spelling "counts" and that careful attention must be paid to syntax. Without the ability to write about their investigative findings, scientists are mute. To a student without a working knowledge of English, science becomes a foreign language. For example, much like its meaning outside of the biological context, *transcription* is the word scientists use to describe the cellular process of making copies of genes to synthesize life-giving proteins.

If there is a mortal sin here, it is the teaching of science disconnected from its history. By so doing we are telling our students that all science is in the present—like the fresh, ever-ready answers of a computer's search engine. As a result, they can't appreciate the frequently long and painful struggle for knowledge engendered by the scientific process. The lack of historical perspective was dramatically demonstrated by one student who asked me if Galileo and Einstein had ever met. To him the twentieth century and the sixteenth were the same. We must, then, somehow separate the centuries. Without perspective, and without the integration of science with other fields, science is like a heart we are trying to keep alive in a bell jar, existing independently of other disciplines which can only elucidate its meaning and sharpen its import.

Scientists are creative individuals, but we often save our exuberance for our research and fail to share it with our students. If we hear the music of the spheres in Mozart's divertimenti for woodwind trio or know why Lewis Thomas thinks a single cell is like a microscopic reflection of all life on earth, we should bring this good news to our students. What we must do is demonstrate that the true scientist is human in the fullest sense.

I smile when I think of Aureolus Philippus Theophrastus Bombastus von Hohenheim, who mercifully dubbed himself Paracelsus. Those familiar with his writings assume he gave us the word *bombast*. He didn't; nonetheless, this sixteenth-century alchemist—and physician of the day—took on his peers with relish and, when he wasn't defending his scientific principles, drank wine with his pupils, rabble-roused, and also found time to establish both the need for accurate diagnosis before treatment begins and the role of chemicals in medical therapy. Paracelsus, Bronowski says, gives us "the transparent sense that a scientific discovery flows from a personality." Knowing about him can only prove that science is not a cold and detached enterprise.

DRAWING STRENGTH FROM YOUNG CURIOSITY

I had thought that teaching college was a challenge until I was asked to give a talk to a group of first- and second-graders in my area of expertise—marine biology.

College teaching had spoiled me. My students are rational adults who usually do what I ask of them. And discipline, blessedly, is usually not an issue. But there is also a constant undertone of passive resistance among university students, a sense that they are in school under duress, champing at the bit to get out into the "real world." Recently, I had to cancel one of my classes due to unforeseen personal circumstances. When I made the apologetic announcement, my students cheered and vacated the room in an instant. (At this point I need to add, in my own defense, that I am considered to be a rather fine teacher.)

Just the opposite happened when I entered the elementary school with my arms full of sea creatures. The little ones, about thirty-five of them, began to jump with excitement. They seemed beside themselves that the object of their anticipation had at long last arrived. Their teacher, Mrs. White, escorted me to a large easy chair, and the children clustered at my feet, eager for the lesson to begin. What more could I ask for as a balm for the ego my own students had unwittingly battered?

I decided to begin simply, with questions of a general nature. "Can any of you name a sea creature that's not a fish?" I asked. Immediately thirty-five hands shot up. I was already wondering who would be the first to say "rock" or "seaweed." I pointed to a little boy, who proclaimed, "Zooplankton!"

It was clear I would have to ratchet up the level of my expectations.

I rummaged in my box of tricks and pulled out a stingray preserved in a clear plastic block, which I held up for all to see. The ooh's and aah's were spontaneous and heartfelt. The children wanted to know every-thing about it: what it ate, how it swam, where I got it. My every de-scription and explication excited greater emotion among them, and in return, they astounded me with their own knowledge. I was face-to-face with the raw cusp of human curiosity, something I experienced only rarely at the college level. Between the ages of seven and eighteen, then, something must happen in the lives of students. In eleven short years they leap from unrestrained enthusiasm for learning to the guarded hope that their teacher will cancel class. To an eighteen-year-old, the teacher is guilty of dictating good taste; whereas, to a seven-year-old, everything simply tastes good.

I continued to draw strength from my interaction with the children. I showed them a sea urchin, a clam, a marine worm, and even a preserved porcupine fish with its spines fully extended.

First-grader: "What happens if you touch it?"

My response: "You can get hurt."

First-grader: "Wow!"

We discussed the anatomy and habits of all my specimens, and still they wanted more.

By the end of an hour my stamina was starting to wane, pitted as it was against the unrelenting physical and emotional energy of children. Like a rubber band pulled taut, they were operating just within the lim-its of tolerance. In the middle of my talk a little boy began to wave his hand wildly, his face a mask of desperation. When I called on him he burst into tears and cried, "I want to go home!" I watched helplessly, still holding the porcupine fish, as Mrs. White swept him up in her arms and comforted him.

Teaching young children was clearly a job with many dimensions: there were thirty-five separate worlds in that classroom, each quivering with boundless energy, each with its own demands, every one of which must be addressed by the teacher ("I lost my lunch money!"). And every moment must be accounted for, the hours packed with one activity after another.

My sea creature talk continued for an hour and a half, ending only because we were up against the dismissal bell. Otherwise there was still a crab and a barnacle in my box, and we could have gone on from there. Or at least they could have. I was ready for recess.

As I gathered my materials together to leave the classroom several children came up to me to tell me how much they had enjoyed the talk or to share experiences of their own ("A shark tried to bite my father!"). A little girl hugged me. A boy shook my hand with the enthusiasm of a presidential candidate. As I left the room they were already receiving instructions for the thank-you notes that would arrive *en masse* in my mailbox a few days later.

The unusual thing about the experience of teaching young children was that they were interested in what I was selling. Despite my affection for my own students, and my dedication to my job, I realized that at the university I was frequently selling the unwanted to the nonbuying. I don't mean this in a cynical way. In a sense, that's the challenge. It's an exercise in conversion: my students doubt that I can interest them in my course and I'm betting that I can. Most of them don't really want to come to class, but they do their best to listen, generally refrain from outbursts, and it has been years since one of my eighteen-year-olds broke down in tears and told me he wanted to go home.

My talk on sea creatures received rave reviews from teacher and students. Mrs. White even suggested that I apply for a position at the elementary school. I was flattered by her faith in my capabilities, but I could do no less than tell her the truth of the matter: her job was much too demanding. When I returned to my own classroom I found my students quietly expectant. "What are we going to talk about today?" a young woman asked. "Zooplankton," I said, still glowing from my triumph with the kids. Several in the class groaned, but I was quick to comfort them. "Don't worry," I said. "It's not complicated. A seven-year-old could understand it."

MY SHORT LESSON ON HOW TO TEACH

I was recently asked by a local high school English teacher to speak to his class about writing. I was flattered and seized the opportunity to indulge myself with creative abandon.

I entered the high school during a change in classes. Almost immediately, I was swept up in a hectic flow of adolescent bodies as they hurried apace to make it to their next class within the prescribed two minutes. I felt like flotsam in a spring torrent and found myself awash in memories of a previous return I had made to high school some twenty years ago, as a wet-behind-the-ears teacher.

In the midseventies I had the good fortune to get a teaching position fresh out of college. In fact, it was at the very all-boys high school I had attended in my hometown in New Jersey. I had not gone through an education curriculum—the principal had hired me on the recommendation of one of his teachers, who had told him, "He has the potential for success." Such was the uncomplicated tenor of the times. As ersatz for the four years of education courses I had bypassed, the principal gave me these sage words of advice: "Don't smile until Christmas."

My assignment was to teach three classes of sophomore biology and one of freshman earth science. In the weeks before school started I went about my preparations with alacrity. I ordered materials, created syllabi, restocked the laboratory, and even wrote my own lab manual. All this for an annual salary of $9,400, which I considered a fortune.

The day before classes commenced, the principal sent an emissary to me in the form of a veteran teacher. The middle-aged man bore a look of sagacious weariness which stated that he had seen it all and it was my job to keep my mouth shut and listen. I felt like a twelve-year-old as I sat before him, taking in his instruction on how to keep a grade book, what constituted an acceptable amount of homework, and the best way to structure a science test. By the time he finished he had covered some twenty topics. He didn't even ask me if I had any questions. I watched as he shuffled to the door. And then he paused, turned, and looked me dead in the eye. "And remember," he said, "don't smile until Christmas."

Overnight the school went from a calm oasis where teachers sedately prepared for the year ahead to a pandemonium of one thousand boys fresh from the long, untethered days of summer. I stood watching them from the window of my classroom—a veritable army streaming through the front entrance. It struck me that I didn't look much older than many of them. For the first time I felt the slightest tinge of nerves. "Don't smile until Christmas," I quietly recited, and it now seemed to make good sense.

I stepped out into the hallway, into the stream of teenagers, and was immediately engulfed. Then, from behind, I felt a heavy hand on my shoulder. "Where are you supposed to be?" a deep voice demanded. I turned about and stared into the stern visage of the principal. "But I'm one of the teachers!" I cried. "Oh," he said, and sailed on to another labor.

Five minutes later I was confronted with thirty sophomores: large, disheveled, already-sweating bodies shifting in their desks, making the wood squeak. They were looking me over, and it seemed that I could already tell which ones would be the troublemakers. I decided to take the principal's advice and give them a tough line.

I told them that anyone who was late for class would be sent straight to the principal's office. I told them that late homework was unacceptable. No one was to talk out of turn, and mutual respect was my primary bylaw. Of course, I couldn't believe that any of this was coming out of the mouth of someone who just a few months ago had planted a thousand fruit flies in his zoology professor's desk drawer.

When I was done my boys were dumbstruck. I had taken no prisoners. And so, having made my point, I felt a faint smile of self-satisfaction blossom on my face. Then a boy named Freddie piped up. "Hey," he said, "ain't you Adrienne's brother?"

Such is the bane of returning to teach in one's hometown.

From that moment on, the year was a struggle for control. But a twenty-two-year-old has a boundless, self-renewing optimism, and every day bore the promise of success. In retrospect, most of my energy went into keeping my charges just this side of chaos, but we did some wonderful things, including setting up a saltwater aquarium and an ant farm, hatching chicks in an incubator, and making a field trip into the country to watch beavers do their work. I was exhausted at the end of every day, but by morning I wanted the classroom as desperately as fresh air.

And then, at year's end, I did an unexpected thing: I left.

I had to. Because I knew that if I stayed another year I would never be able to pull myself away from those kids, and I needed to know what other doors were open to me.

As I stood before Mr. Phippen's expository writing class the other day, it all rushed back upon me: the students' eagerness as well as their disinterest; the joys and the dilemmas; the days when things went like clockwork, and those which defied my best efforts to bring the class to heel.

My stint as a guest speaker renewed my estimation of high school teaching: it is a special vocation, and I sometimes wonder how long I might have stuck with it had I not needed to be elsewhere, despite the twin handicaps of being Adrienne's brother and having the alarming inclination to smile before Christmas.

MARTIAN LIFE? YE OF TOO MUCH FAITH

It is ironic that indications of Martian life should manifest themselves now, in 1996, an election year, a time when terrans are hard at work proving that intelligent life, at least, does not exist on Earth.

The alacrity with which otherwise-reputable scientists have rushed to proclaim the existence of fossilized microbes in a putatively Martian meteorite is enough to awaken recollections of the "cold fusion" fiasco of recent memory.

For the uninformed, the hubbub is about a rock which is said to have fallen to earth some thirteen thousand years ago. It is green, although it came from the red planet. It looks like a human liver, albeit a small one, weighing in at four and a half pounds. Electron microscopy—an honorable enterprise—has revealed what look like petrified bacteria deep inside the stone. Based on this visual evidence, a committee of NASA scientists has announced, with minimal restraint, that these tiny structures represent life-forms which flourished at a time when Mars was a kinder and gentler place to live.

The business of science is skepticism. So what happened here? I've seen the photographs of the meteorite's innards, and I, too, could interpret the tiny tubules as microbes, if that's what I wanted them to be. But I feel less strongly about the possibility of their representing ancient life-forms than I do about the probability that they are not.

Science has waxed poetic before, and on more than one occasion. I have already mentioned the example of cold fusion, which still has its loyalists. There was also "polywater." In 1968 the first reports appeared in reputable scientific journals that an alternate form of water had been discovered, more viscous than the regular stuff. For four years the fear grew that if polywater were to escape from the laboratory it would proselytize normal water, ending life on earth as we know it. In the end it turned out that polywater was simply water with impurities.

"Mitogenic rays" were another orthodoxy foisted upon unwitting observers by legitimate scientists. The idea here was that plants—such as onions—gave off growth-stimulating rays which affected the other onions around them, "unless a plate of glass were placed between them." Although the existence of these mysterious rays was eventually disproved, papers continued to be published for decades.

The subject of extraterrestrial life is a touchy one. Next to Darwin, there is probably nothing that needles fundamentalists more than this dread prospect. But consider, for a moment, the advent of a *decisive* determination of life beyond Earth. It would, of course, suggest that humans are not the only tourists on the galactic hayride, but are sharing space with other creatures, perhaps humbler, or—gulp—possibly more advanced than we are. There are those who believe that this would cause a titanic shift in the way humans think about themselves. But I am not among them. On the day after the extraterrestrials are confirmed, I expect that Pizza Hut will still have the same menu, the Democrats and Republicans will continue to have at it, and that Wal-Mart will continue to alter the landscape undeterred.

Perhaps even more amazing than the discovery of squiggles in the Martian rock is the existence of a name for the enterprise of studying life in space. It's called "exobiology." For the moment, it is a scam, since we don't know of any life in space. Exobiologists, then, are well paid for studying something which, so far as we know, doesn't exist.

But they are perched in anxious anticipation of their day, which may or may not have arrived. The message here is to hold one's breath and not let it out quite yet. That there is something in the Mars rock is beyond doubt. That it was once living is worthy of doubt. In fact, doubting it is much more scientific than the alleluias which have been echoing through the press and for which scientists should feel deeply abashed.

If and when these Martian bacteria are validated, I will continue to hold my breath for something bigger and better. I have often imagined that perhaps, eons ago, the greenery of the Earth was seeded by immense extraterrestrial beings and that our fair planet served as their garden in the galactic countryside. In the interim, *Homo sapiens* evolved. One day these giants will return, and when they do they are liable to exclaim, "Damn, we've got humans!" Then they'll spray.

And that will be the end of us.

I teach biology at a small college in central Maine. As part of the course, students are required to write essays in which they summarize and interpret their laboratory findings. For most of the students, this type of writing is a new experience, and I find that my written corrections and comments often take up as much space as the assignments themselves.

The problem with writing comments in margins and between lines is that, even while I am at it, I realize that much of what I write will not be read by my students. As testament to this, I have often found essays in the wastebasket—deposited there before the students took the time to read and understand my corrections.

Surely Socrates would have been disappointed by such a response. But then again, he would probably have been disappointed in this approach to teaching as well.

In this light, I decided years ago to radically reform the way I assess my students' work. In essence, I decided to take as Socratic an approach as I could with a class of thirty-five.

Realizing how attentive my students generally are when I speak to them, I designed a way for them to take my voice (along with its sage counsel) home: instead of writing my thoughts on their papers, I would record them on tape.

At first my students were apprehensive about this scheme. Their greatest fear was that they would also have to speak on the tapes. When I assured them it would be a one-way street, they grew more accepting of the idea. A week later they handed in their first essays along with the requisite blank cassettes.

I took the thirty-five tapes and papers home in a cardboard box. That evening I spread them out on the living room floor. And then I commenced to read and record.

As I adjusted to this new way of doing things I found that I could be both more personal and detailed in my comments. When I gave the first tapes and papers back, the students received them with bated breath, regarding their returned work with a mixture of dread and curiosity.

Later that day I got an inkling of the impact of my commentaries. While on my way to the library I saw some of my students huddled around a table in the lounge area. And then I heard what sounded like my own voice coming out of their midst. They were all listening intently to one of the tapes, periodically remarking at something I had said.

Without alerting them to my presence, I snuck into the library and tended to my business.

As the weeks went by both the students and I became more comfortable with this tape approach. Some of them even began to have fun with it, recording fragments of their favorite (and invariably awful) music, which I didn't erase, but rather retained as a cacophonous overture to my commentary on their work. Others actually found the courage to say a few syllables. One student managed, "This is fun," while another told an endless joke, whose punch line still eludes me.

As for the papers, they were generally of average quality, but there was a student named Daniel whose early papers were nothing short of abysmal. I wasn't even sure I was reading English. I felt that if I tackled all of Daniel's deficiencies at once I would discourage him, so I decided to try to bring him around by degrees: grammar one week, punctuation the next, then complete sentences, and so on.

When I returned Daniel's first tape he accepted it with palpable trepidation. He looked up at me without saying a word, but his eyes conveyed a sense of "I know I'm not good at this, but I really am trying."

Daniel commuted to school from quite a distance. He lived far out in the country, deep in the woods. My take on him was that he came from an impoverished background, but yes, he was a hard worker who had just not had access to the necessary means of study.

He seemed to be profiting from the tapes, though, because with each passing week his work visibly improved. By semester's end he was actually writing coherent and sometimes creative essays. I finally took him aside to tell him how proud I was of him. "I hope the tapes helped you," I remarked.

"I learned a lot from them," he assured me with genuine enthusiasm. "Despite the cold."

"The cold?" I echoed, not sure of his meaning.

That's when I learned how hard Daniel had really worked.

"Yeah," he said. "I don't have my own tape recorder, but there's one in my dad's truck. So at night I go out there, start it up, and sit and listen to the tapes."

The image of this earnest student huddled in a pickup, deep in the dark and snow of the Maine woods, listening to my voice, totally unmanned me. If not for the tapes, I might never have known how seriously Daniel took his education. They also allowed me to touch this student in a way my written comments never could.

That was eight years ago. I'm still doing the tapes, but the service they provide to my students occasionally pales against the insights they yield into how truly good-hearted and deserving these people are.

In a profession that can too easily become routine, such thoughts need to be cast in bronze, or at least recorded on cassette.

A FRENCH TUTOR'S FIRST LESSON

I recently harkened to a call for volunteer tutors from my town's middle school. "I have three seventh-grade boys," said the enthusiastic teacher over the phone, "who desperately need a French tutor."

My spirits flagged a bit. "But I don't speak French," I told her.

"Don't worry," she assured me. "It's very basic. In any case, these kids would benefit from a positive male role model."

I halfheartedly discussed details of the arrangement with her (two one-hour sessions per week) and then signed off with a weakly enunciated "*Au revoir,*" which represented almost the sum total of my French know-how.

What had I gotten myself into? As a Spanish speaker, I took some comfort in the realization that I could build some bridges between the two languages. But when it came to free expression I would be hopelessly adrift.

Ironically, I had been given French instruction in grammar school in the early sixties. This consisted of a grainy black-and-white TV program beamed into Mrs. Cheriko's fourth-grade class by the infant National Educational Television system. I still recall watching, along with thirty of my classmates, the antics of Jacques and Marie, two French children to whom we were expected to relate. The goal, as explained by Mrs. Cheriko, was to repeat everything these children said.

Most of it went right over my head. Mrs. Cheriko was of little help because she didn't speak French either and was learning along with us. All I remember of the program is the opening "*Bonjour,*" and the closing—you got it—"*Au revoir.*"

And now I was en route to my first tutoring session, feeling more like I was on my way to a lunar landing, not knowing exactly what I would find once I had set down.

When I arrived at the school, Mme. Lutein, my contact teacher, introduced me to Mike, Peter, and Ryan. The boys only half-acknowledged me, which I perceived as a good thing, for maybe they would not take great notice of my French—or lack of it—either.

I led the boys to a small classroom and spent the first few minutes of our forty-five-minute session just chatting in an attempt to get to know them. They all agreed that French was difficult for them. "What's the hardest part?" I asked.

Ryan was the most loquacious and immediately volunteered, "The words!"

Mike and Peter chimed in, "Yeah, learning new words."

I had come prepared for this. "Okay," I said as I divided a dozen index cards among the boys. "Each of you look in your book and pick out some French words you want to learn. Write a word down on each of your cards."

I looked on as my young charges went to work, scratching away with their pencils for ten minutes. After they were done I spread the cards out on the floor about six feet from where they sat. Then I took a rubber ball from my pocket and handed it to Mike. "Okay," I said. "Bounce the ball and try to hit a card. If you do, and you can pronounce the word, you win the card."

The boys went at this with alacrity. They shared the ball, called each other's hits and misses, and listened carefully as vocabulary words were pronounced. Of course, I had little idea whether their pronunciations were accurate but assumed that their consensus on any given word was probably close to the mark.

Before I knew it our session was over. I drilled them one last time on the new words, without benefit of the cards, and was surprised at how much they had retained. As they left the room Peter turned to me and, in all innocence, remarked, "You don't speak French, do you?" I admitted that I didn't. His response: "Cool."

As I lingered in thought I realized what had just happened in our little classroom. I had been cornered into doing what a good teacher is supposed to do: not so much imparting knowledge as facilitating the search for it.

With renewed confidence I hurried home, where I took out my resume and, under "Work Experience," ceremoniously added the words *French Tutor*. Why not? By the end of the school year, some five months hence, who knows how much I will have learned from my students?

One of the high points of the semester is when I indulge one of my great pleasures—collecting seaweed for my students.

In poetry, art, and song, the sea has been celebrated as having unsurpassed beauty. But, truth to tell, there is much in the ocean that is downright ugly—to the uninitiated.

Take seaweeds, for example. They don't flower, they're slimy, and their spectrum of colors is limited to red, brown, and green. Even some of their names sound disagreeable: *Fucus, Chondrus, Ulva.*

My students' experiences with seaweed do nothing to ennoble it. They relate childhood episodes of splatting their siblings with gobs of the stuff. Others describe having smelled it rotting on the beach. Now and then I encounter the intrepid soul who has eaten it, vowing never to do so again.

To me, my students' attitudes toward seaweed represent nothing less than a challenge. To take something which at first blush seems uninteresting at best and reveal the beauty within is, for me, a deeply satisfying aspect of teaching.

As I drive through the low, snow-covered hills along the Penobscot River, my anticipation steadily heightens as the river widens toward the bay. I don't know what excites me more, the seaweed or the idea of being absolutely alone on a Maine beach in the very heart of winter. Perhaps it is some intangible combination of the two.

I arrive at Blue Hill Falls at low tide—heaven for the marine biologist in search of algae. Some specimens can withstand exposure to air until the tide rises again, but others must stay submerged. The ebb tide allows me to get within arm's length of these holdouts. If I'm lucky, I'll return with a bucket containing sixteen or so different species.

My students find it hard to believe that some biologists—called phycologists—spend their professional lives studying the seaweeds. When I was an undergraduate I actually hobnobbed with a professor who had discovered a completely new species. He named it after his wife, calling it *Patricia elegans.* A decided improvement over *Fucus.*

I sit down on a large rock and pull on my waders. I am surrounded by seaweeds. Upbeach are the rockweeds, high but not quite dry. At my feet are leathery sheets of devil's apron, brown and perforated. In the tidepool not five feet from where I am sitting are tufts of green tubeweed and the pinkish, delicately branched *Corallina.*

Before I embarked upon this collecting trip I dramatized the effort for my students, portraying it as something of a safari. In fact, on some of my trips I have gone to heroic lengths to retrieve that perfect specimen. I once descended into a cleft in a sheer granite outcropping right at the water's edge at Schoodic Point, a place known for its aggressive storm surges and breaking waves. I wanted to retrieve a specimen of a sheer, pleated red seaweed called "laver" (*Porphyra umbilicalis*). My young son stood slack-jawed as I strained after the alga with an outstretched arm, managing to seize it in my fingertips and scramble from the cleft just as a massive breaker exploded at my heels.

Earlier in the course I had primed my students for their first informed contact with seaweeds by telling them some amazing facts about the plants. For example, a single blade of giant kelp can grow to two hundred feet. Sargassum weed, one of the few unattached seaweeds, is the trysting place for the American eel. And if they look at the list of ingredients on a carton of good-quality ice cream, they'll see carrageenan, a seaweed extract that lends smoothness to the product.

Like anything else in nature, seaweeds are at their best in their native habitat. At low tide one is able to look down and see them splayed out like angelhair or shifting about like mopheads. In the gentlest current they sway at ease, as if showing off the latest fashions. When I remove them from the water they collapse into slippery, amorphous clumps. But when I drop them into my bucket of seawater, they blossom again, still beautifully alive, renewing their graceful dances.

The grandmother of a friend of mine was a marine biologist early in the twentieth century—a time when it provided a livelihood for few men, let alone women. When she passed away she left her granddaughter a unique and lovely gift from the sea: a set of individually framed seaweeds which she had ever-so-carefully lifted from the water on sheets of paper so as to preserve some semblance of their natural form for posterity. The name of each specimen was lovingly hand-lettered in the clear and flowing script of a bygone age.

My students don't realize how much they know about the seaweeds already. Before I left for the coast, we reviewed their characteristics in depth. The fact that seaweeds have no roots because they get their nutrients from the seawater that surrounds them. Some seaweeds are edible: dulse and kelp, for example. Other seaweeds live out their lives attached only to other seaweeds. The dense mats and forests of seaweeds in the ocean's shallows provide both food and a refuge for a tremendous array of sea creatures, juvenile and adult.

The incoming tide augurs the end of my collecting trip. In my bucket I have fifteen different species. Not bad. I pack up my things and begin the drive back to school. When I arrive I will fill fifteen fingerbowls with cold, clear seawater and reverentially transfer a seaweed into each one.

When my students enter the laboratory they will set to work, touching, examining, sketching. I feel as if I have prepared a feast for them, and I will stand on the threshold, looking on with deep satisfaction as something that was ill-thought-of, or even un-thought-of, slowly becomes extraordinary for them.

This is teaching's essence—and its deepest reward.

LET US PRAISE THE BOLD MOLDS

It's that time of the school year again, the point in my college biology course when I must scramble, in the dead of winter, to grow fungi for my students.

To most, it's not a very alluring notion, but to a biologist, the fungi are not only intriguing, but also beautiful.

Delicate as cotton wisps or tough as leather, each species of fungus has its own very narrow range of growing conditions—temperature, humidity, light, and nature of the substrate—which allow it to blossom forth, often explosively. Who hasn't awoken on a damp autumn morning to find the lawn, or that shaded patch under a pine tree, studded with mushrooms that weren't there the day before?

When conditions are just right, fungi will not be daunted. Many years back there was a New Jersey man who discovered mushrooms breaking through the hardened asphalt of his driveway. The fellow dug at them, poured lime over them, and even set them on fire, but still they grew. They had to. It was their time. In a contest between man and fungus, the outcome is seldom in doubt.

Molds, mildews, mushrooms. Fungi all. What they have in common is that they are composed of tiny fibers—hyphae—which in some places are packed tightly together, as in the mushroom, and in other places are highly diffuse, as in some species of bread mold. A determined and patient mycologist (one who studies fungi) once measured the growing tips of all the hyphae of a bread mold and found that, in a single night, it had grown an astounding *one kilometer.*

I often sing the praises of the fungi to my students. Once they get over the unappealing sound of the word, most of them warm to these organisms. Neither plant nor animal, they emulate both: they often look like plants, but, like animals, they must get their food elsewhere, usually from dead or decaying organic matter. Ever wonder why the forest isn't littered with the fallen trunks of dead trees? 'Tis fungi that germinate and spread as soon as (and sometimes before) the sap of these trees has ceased to flow. In fact, even while these trees were young and thriving, their bows aloft, their leaves thirsting for the sun, they were literally blanketed with the microscopic spores of fungi. These spores had been biding their time, waiting for their opportunity to return the wood's nutrients to the earth whence they came.

In these days preceding our chapter on the fungi, I find myself busily preparing specimens for my students' study and, I hope, delight. Fungi are big and small, pale and brilliantly colored, thready and buttonlike. Most important, they will "attack" anything of an organic nature. In fact, there is evidence they will grow on just about anything that contains carbon, whether it was once living or not. A friend of mine who had moved to Galveston from the Midwest once left her Texas home for a week and made the mistake of turning off the air conditioning. Upon her return, she discovered that fungi had eaten away the rubber seal on the door of her refrigerator, then had begun to consume the food that lay within. Talk about opportunists.

On those occasions when detractors sniff at my affinity for the fungi, I remind myself—and them—that I am in good company. The poet Frederick George Scott once wrote (albeit in a state of despondency), "Day by day the moulded smell / of this fungus-blistered cell." And the Nobel laureate Seamus Heaney, in his poem "Personal Helicon," spoke fondly of them:

> As a child, they could not keep me from wells
> And old pumps with buckets and windlasses.
> I loved the dark drop, the trapped sky, the smells
> Of waterweed, fungus and dank moss.

And for those whose reading is restricted to whatever glimmers on the computer screen, there is a wonderful Web site called "The Norwegian Fungus of the Month."

I take a piece of bread, some orange rind, a dab of marmalade, and even a piece of leather from an old shoe. Each of these I place in its own petri dish. Add a mist of water from an atomizer before setting the covers down. Then I put these dishes in the darkness of a paper bag and set them on top of the refrigerator, a place of subtle warmth. After a week I open the bag and—voilà!—the desert has blossomed like a rose, or rather, like a mold, four separate species to be exact, in colors ranging from black to orange to blue-green.

I have my fungi, and I couldn't be happier.

FINDING "AHS" IN THE OOZE

There is a striking contrast between the effects of winter snow and spring rain. In the former case, snow is a soporific: its message is one of repose as it encourages the gentle drop of leaves, the southbound flight of the robin and the migration underground of various small animals.

But rain is a life-giver, an awakener, a quickener. It comes down by the bucket as spring showers, cascading from rooftops, dripping from the sopping canopy of the forest and coursing briskly along curbs. This is water's spring drama. But I find myself more deeply drawn to its denouement: its understated collection as temporary places in the forest known as vernal pools.

Here in Maine we are in the thick of vernal pool season. Those of us "in the know" seize this window of opportunity to seek out the low places, the depressions along roadcuts, the hollows in the pine groves, the quiet, seasonal pools that differentiate themselves from ponds by their diminutive size and their lack of an outlet. Vernal pools are there for only a while, and there are certain creatures that are even more keenly attuned to their transient nature than we are. In fact, their lives depend upon vernal pools.

I had almost forgotten what time of year it was when, a couple of weeks back, I took my college biology class on a short field trip into the forest. Our interest was in the trees themselves, so our eyes were directed upward. As we emerged from the woods, though, I caught a glint of sunlight off to the left of the path we were treading. Suddenly the field trip took a detour as I called my students together. "Look good and close at it now," I directed them, "because tomorrow it might not be here."

Vernal pools do not, of course, disappear overnight, but their lack of staying power makes every day of their existence a gift. That white pine over there will always serve as a landmark, and that boulder deposited ten thousand years ago by the last glacier will likely persist for another ten, but this pool is totally dependent on the vagaries of the seasons. During these cool, wet days of spring, vernal pools lie in state, often underlain by bedrock or the tough, unbroken soil called hardpan, which prevents the water from percolating deeper into the earth. But come summer, with the advent of hot weather and a merciless sun, they evaporate without a trace.

So what did I want my students to note about the pool we were hovering over? The scene itself, pastoral though it was, had limited interest. "Look closer," I told them, "and see who can tell me where the biology comes in."

There were a few cursory comments about insects and plants, but these organisms generally abide the vernal pools; they don't depend upon them. I squatted down at the water's edge and reached in. A moment later I gently lifted out a greenish mass with the consistency of Jello. Embedded within was the prize: the pea-size eggs of some amphibian whose rhythms are perfectly in sync with the annual coming and going of the vernal pool.

My students paid due respect to the egg mass, but few had any inclination to touch it. For my part, I didn't want to put it down. It is the lot of the hard-boiled biology teacher that he lives for the "oohs" and "ahs" from his students that make science teaching so rewarding. But in this case we were at semester's end, wrapping things up as it were, and more than one student took the opportunity to check his watch.

So where does the teacher go when he wants elation, wonder, and a wholesale return of enthusiasm for one's modest efforts?

Kindergarten, of course.

A few days later I returned to the vernal pool with my six-year-old son, Anton, and two of his buddies. But for the life of me I couldn't find any egg masses. Could they all have hatched? Or was the sun not at the right angle for illuminating the shaded water? I decided to put my diminutive biologists to work, describing in detail what we were looking for. Within five minutes my son was squatting poolside, with an egg mass overflowing his small hands. As he, I, and his cohorts gathered around, we gazed deep into the jelly, noting the developing young, each in its own little egg. "Salamanders," I whispered, and they echoed my pronouncement with glee. We deposited the eggs in a pickle jar and made off with our precious gleaning.

The next morning I arrived at my son's kindergarten class with micro-scope in hand. We set up the scope, focused it on an egg mass, and the munchkins lined up, beside themselves with anticipation. The exclama-tions were enough to fuel my pedagogue's conceit for many, many more miles of teaching.

In a week or so, once the salamanders had hatched, we would return them to the vernal pool to complete their metamorphosis, and to insure that, generation upon generation, the drama would be played out for tomorrow's kindergartners, and for biology teachers still willing to get their feet wet when winter turns to spring.

A Son from Russia

I am in John F. Kennedy International Airport waiting in line to check in for Aeroflot flight 316 to Moscow. All the other people in line are Russians. The men are thickset, sweating in dark, baggy suits. Their faces are wide enough to recline in. The women wear outsized bracelets and earrings that jangle when they move. Their faces are caked with makeup.

Someone pushes me from behind. One of the thickset men. "Move up!" he barks. I comply.

Everyone is talking—the harsh palatalizations of the Russian language sound like water rushing past my ears. It is a breathless language. Perhaps the Russian Bible reads, "In the beginning there was the paragraph."

I kick my Lands' End duffle along as the line inches forward. The Russians have no Lands' End duffles. They have no suitcases. No valises. They have cardboard boxes, tied and taped to hold them together. As I stand in line, I watch as an immense roll of duct tape is passed from hand to hand to reinforce the boxes, which are bursting at the seams from being kicked along the floor as if they were Lands' End duffles. I consider this to be the last vestige of the old Soviet socialism: everyone is entitled to the roll of duct tape. Except me. When the duct tape reaches the man in front of me, he passes it over my head.

I find myself offended by these people. They look dangerous. They cast no shadows, because they are shadows. They look as if they could have their hands in my pocket at any moment. And yet my prospective son is Russian. In eighteen years will he be standing in an Aeroflot line in New York, smoking black tobacco, fingering a roll of duct tape and filling a suit that could also serve as a double-breasted pup tent?

The adoption is not yet a done deal. It cannot even be presumed, even though I am traveling to Russia at the invitation of the adoption authorities there. I already know what my son looks like. The agency sent me a four-minute video in which he recites a poem from memory and chews gum. He is a small seven-year-old, and in the video he is wearing what I am told are his very best clothes: a Mickey Mouse pullover from which the red dye has run, a collared shirt, and a pair of black-and-white–checked pants. Although I had steeled myself against it, I fell in love with him almost immediately. So now my heart is committed while my head tells me not to jump the gun. My task at the moment is not to pretend that Alexei Viktorovich Sidorov, age seven, is my son. My task is to kick my Lands' End duffle along the floor.

I have been standing in line for thirty minutes and have almost reached the ticket counter. Suddenly, six people come out of nowhere and pile in front of me. They push me back to make room for themselves. I stumble into a man who looks like Nikita Khrushchev. He pushes me forward. The people in front of me push me back. Several Russians somewhere else in the line shout their objections. Then the line calms, the conversations resume, and the duct tape continues its rounds.

During my preadoptive parenting classes I had mentioned that I felt prepared for anything in my son's personality. But now I found myself hoping that he would not be a pusher.

I have been standing in line for forty-five minutes. The people who cut in front of me are now being waited on. I have to go to the bathroom. Desperately. I turn to the man behind me. The one who looks like Khrushchev. Although he had pushed me earlier he seems rather benign. He does not look as if he would take off his shoe and beat it on a table at the United Nations. "Do you speak English?" I ask him.

He takes the cigarette from his mouth. "*Da.*"

I ask him if he would be kind enough to watch my Lands' End duffle while I go to the bathroom. "*Da.*"

I am gone ten minutes. When I return I notice that the line has advanced a tad and that the man who looks like Khrushchev has been kicking my Lands' End duffle along for me. I rejoin the line. "Thank you," I say. He nods. "Why are you going to Russia?" he asks.

I am struck by his English, which is almost unaccented. I tell him that I am adopting a little Russian boy.

The man removes the cigarette from his mouth and puts his hand on my shoulder. I can feel the heat from the glowing tip behind my ear. "Thank you," he says, "for adopting one of these children." And then he smiles at me as if apologizing for his entire country.

The next thing I know he is handing me the roll of duct tape, which he has just received from the woman behind him. "Pass it along," he says, and I hand the roll to the person in front of me.

I suddenly feel that I belong in this line. That I have been accepted into the circle of duct tape passers.

"Next."

It is the ticket agent. I pick up my duffle and take one giant step forward. And then another.

I am standing on the seventh-floor balcony of an apartment building overlooking the heart of Moscow. It is a dark city, some might say grim. It looks and feels as if it has been worn down to its bare bones: broken sidewalks, cracked façades, weeds rooted in the very mortar. This city is not easy to look at. So I avert my eyes, and they settle on a little boy sleeping in the convertible bed inside the apartment. His name is Alyosha. He is seven. With every rise and fall of his chest, Moscow, the used, broken city, is renewed for me a thousand times. A dark place has given me light in the form of my adoptive son.

Alyosha has been my son for only two days, but I have been waiting three years for him. That's when I began the adoption process, three years ago, before I even knew of his existence. Never in my imaginings did I think that I would one day be so far from home, counting my son's respirations, counting the hours until we would board a plane for America, a place which he had little conception of. "Alyosha," I had said through a translator as I knelt before him at the orphanage and helped him with his socks. "What do you know about America?" His reply was immediate: "I will have all the gum I want."

Most people adopt infants or toddlers, so that as much of their history as possible will be that given to them by their parents. But Alyosha, as an older child, carries an effulgence of native culture: his memories of orphanage life in the once-closed city of Tula; the large, gracious, doting Russian women who have cared for him here; the aromatic, fatty Russian foods he loves; and the crown jewel of his experience—the language—that impossible, expressive, explosive Russian language which sometimes separates us like a wall but also summons us to heroic lengths as we attempt to communicate with each other.

I have been in Russia for two weeks. But it wasn't until the fourth day that I was brought to see Alyosha. My Russian contact drove me through one hundred miles of a country struggling to get back on its feet after years of internal neglect: pitted roadways, crumbling bridges, warped roofs. It made me recall what someone had once said about the Soviet Union, that she was a Third World country with a First World army.

We finally came to an orphanage overgrown with weeds, its play areas knee-high in goldenrod and other opportunists. Once inside, I stood in the middle of a near-empty room, hovering precipitously, realizing that this was the light at the end of a three-year-long tunnel of scrutiny, disappointment, false hopes, grinding progress, and the frenetic accumulation of document after document intended to certify me a good risk as an adoptive parent. There were moments when I had told myself, "It's so much easier to have a kid the natural way. Nobody asks any questions." But for me, a single man, a biological child was not a ready option. I now recognized these as idle thoughts, for I realized that Alyosha would be as much mine as if he carried my genes.

A door opened on the other side of the room, and I rose up on my toes in anticipation. No one appeared. Then the door closed and I settled back down. I looked to my liaison, who nodded reassuringly. The door opened again. This time a woman came out, her hand on the shoulder of a little boy just awakened from sound sleep. He was wearing blue shorts, a T-shirt, and socks. Rubbing his eyes, he shuffled over to me. "Do you know who this is?" asked his caretaker. Alyosha raised his head and squinted. "Papa?" he said matter-of-factly, but with the barest hint of "What took you so long?"

I gave Alyosha a Pez dispenser and a pack of candy, things as alien to him as his image of America. After a few moments' scrutiny he began to fill it with candy (a sure sign of intelligence, for Pez dispensers are notoriously difficult to load). Then he took my hand and showed me the bedroom he shared with seven other boys. After getting him dressed, we walked out of the building and visited his playground, then the refectory, where he pointed out the place where he sat and ate his meals. We covered his whole world in twenty minutes. Everything he knew, all the people who were familiar to him, were within touching distance. I wondered at that moment how profound the grief of his parting would be.

At the end of our first meeting I knelt before Alyosha and told him I would return for him in a week. "Will you miss me?" I asked. He raised his eyes to meet mine. "I won't miss you," he said. "But I'll wait for you." I thought this an excellent and appropriate answer.

I had thought that my meeting Alyosha had put the imprimatur on the adoption. But it had been only a speculative viewing: I was informed that I could still decline to adopt him. Were there people who actually traveled to Russia, met their adoptive sons or daughters, and then begged off? It had happened more than once, I was told, but for me it was beyond imagining. I am unmanned by any child who can load a Pez dispenser with such dexterity.

I had hoped that the worst of the paperwork was behind me, but it was just the opposite. The ensuing week was filled with apprehension and sleepless nights. So many documents had yet to be signed and sealed. The task was to track down the various ministers and other signatories. Thus began a maddening round of visits and delays and attempts to reach authorities over phone lines eternally troubled by static, low volume, and outright lack of service. In Russia authority follows a person wherever he or she goes (even to the grave, I had feared, when one minister we were scheduled to see was out sick). Authority is so coveted that it is never delegated, so if a person is not in the office, one has no choice but to retreat and return another day. By midweek, with the passport and upper-eschelon signatures still to be gotten, I began to despair of ever seeing Alyosha again. "It is not yet time to panic," my liaison counseled. I gave that confidence a desperate embrace.

At the eleventh hour, just before all the government offices in Tula closed for the weekend, the clouds broke, and one by one the requisite documents came rolling in. In fact, they fluttered into my hands as if heaven-sent. It led me to suspect that the whole tense scheme had been concocted as a way of seeing how much I could take. If it had been a test of some sort I seemed to have passed. The news that Alyosha was now my son was almost incidental; it was certainly anticlimactic. A man in a military uniform handed me Alyosha's passport. "Take care of your son," he said as he shook my hand and smiled.

One week after first meeting Alyosha I returned to the orphanage to pick him up. It was a wet, dismal afternoon, the pendulous branches of the silver maples sweeping the ground. I entered Alyosha's building and found forty or so boys running around, making the best of a rainy day. When they saw me they froze, knowing why I had come. And then he appeared, running at me. Alyosha leaped into my arms and gave me a bone-crushing hug. "Get dressed," I said. "Home?" he asked in Russian. I nodded.

There ensued a group photo and the passing out of much-prized bubble gum. I handed Alyosha a teddy bear, the only thing, next to the Pez dispenser, that he had ever owned. He placed his free hand in mine and turned once to his friends to wave good-bye. We left the building, and he never looked back.

I want to sleep, but I cannot take my eyes from my son. I am not sure I am yet convinced that he is really mine. I sense, with the faith of a dreamer, that the best days, for both Alyosha and me, lie ahead, in a land brimming with bubble gum and other good things. I turn my eyes to

Moscow again. It is 11:00 P.M. and the sun is still shining brilliantly, reflected here and there by the gold leaf of onion domes. It is as if Russia is providing all the light and time I need to discover the beauty beyond the shadows. But when I consider what it has given me, I realize that I already have.

A MONEY-SHY SON MAKES A SAVVY ALLOWANCE

When my son turned ten last month he made a momentous request for an allowance.

I say momentous because up to that point, Alyosha had literally wanted nothing to do with money. He liked to have things, of course, but he didn't like to do the actual buying. Whenever a relative tucked a dollar or two into a birthday or Christmas card, he'd reflexively hand the money over to me, saying, "You take care of it." My attempts to encourage him to at least learn something about the handling of money were met with total disinterest.

Where, then, did the zeal for an allowance come from?

It turns out that the subject had been a hot one in school one day. So with all the enthusiasm of the new convert he returned home with a mission.

After careful negotiations, we arrived at a figure of two dollars a week. Then we shook hands on it. As I turned away he cleared his throat. "Dad," he said as I looked back at him with raised eyebrows, "the two dollars?"

Oh. So soon? I reached into my wallet and pulled out two worn bills, which I handed over with great aplomb. He admired them for a few moments before slipping them into his pocket. And off he went, flush with his first mazuma.

Then came the great disillusionment.

Later that day we were in a convenience store and Alyosha was cruising the aisles, wide-eyed. "Dad," he said, "will you buy me a soda?"

My response was the only one possible in light of our new financial relationship. "Do you have your allowance?" I asked him.

He nodded cautiously, his face showing unease.

"Well, that's what it's for," I told him.

To make a long story short, he didn't buy his soda and decided that for the balance of the afternoon he wouldn't talk to me either.

That evening there was an opening for me to explain to my son the nature of an allowance. "I'll continue to buy you the things you need," I told him as he listened with the focus of an attorney, "but an allowance is for the things you want." (Of course, there were certain clauses and subsections where the spirit of giving prevailed, such as birthdays and holidays.)

This was the beginning of a long series of debates, discussions, and philosophical probings into the nature of the allowance. I had to keep reminding myself that Alyosha didn't fully understand the concept yet because he had literally made a leap from total disdain for money to a desire to have some of his own. His hard lesson was that an allowance was not simply the accumulation of surplus wealth in his cookie can, but a resource which would allow him to meet—and ration—his material wants. The boon for me was that, as the concept of an allowance matured for my son over time, I was no longer in the position of being expected to automatically fork over money for every doodad and trinket he spied on store shelves. "Resources are limited," I told my barely comprehending son one evening as I tucked him into bed. "Money is a resource. We spend a little to buy a little, and we save a little for another day."

The upshot was that only once did Alyosha squander his entire allowance on the day he had received it. He quickly recouped and learned to manage his money well. One day when we were out shopping together I paused to look over some kitchen utensils while Alyosha rummaged through a bargain box of cartoon videos. Next to him was another boy, perhaps a year younger, screaming at his mother and pulling at her coat, demanding that she buy him one of the videos. She resisted valiantly, reciting *no* three or four times. Finally, she gave in, shoved the video into her son's arms, and they went off together. What struck me about this disheartening scene was the way my son had regarded the pair. He had studied them blankly, as if observing people speaking a foreign language. As for me, I felt liberated.

I went over to Alyosha and put my hand on his shoulder as he looked at the tape he held in his hand. "Should I get this?" he asked. I shrugged. "Is it something you really want?" I asked. He nodded. "Then that's what your allowance is for," I told him.

After Alyosha made his purchase we headed home. On the way we stopped for gas at a general store. After I filled up I went into the store to pay. As I reached for my wallet I experienced one of the most singularly desperate feelings in the world: the empty pocket. Had I lost it? Had it been stolen? Or had I simply left it at home?

I ran back to the car, where my son was serenely reading the package description on his tape. "Alyosha," I said, leaning through the window, "I can't find my wallet. Do you have five dollars you can lend me?"

He looked up at me and blinked. Then he took his money out of his pocket and unfolded five crisp singles. As I reached for the bills, he suddenly pulled them away. "Wait a minute," he said, as I hovered between desperation and embarrassment.

"Yes? What is it?"

"Is it for something you need or something you want?"

I firmed my lip, trying to suppress a smile. "It's for something we both need," I told him.

He handed the money to me, and I set off to pay for the gas. My boy had learned his lesson well, and he had tempered it with mercy.

A SON BEGINS TO WIDEN HIS ORBIT

My son's relationship to me has always been that of a moon orbiting its planet: he periodically strays to transit my dark side, but on the whole he has been sweet, mannered, modest in his wants, and tolerably dependent. I have often described him as a "low-maintenance" kid.

It seems like only yesterday that he was a seven-year-old in a Russian orphanage. When I went to pick him up, he leapt into my arms and never looked back. And now, although he is small for his age, I see him perched for the explosion that will replace the boy with the young man.

In a few days my son will turn twelve.

I can hardly believe it. But though I struggle at times to retain the image of the little boy I've known, reality has ways of making itself felt. In the matter of my son, there have been undeniable signs.

Alyosha recently informed me that his room is no longer big enough. He sat me down at the kitchen table and sketched an addition that would stick out from the side of the house like a poop deck and have a fireman's pole descending to ground level against the advent of a quick escape.

This was followed by his request for a boom box (or is it boombox?). When Alyosha asked for the device I was dumbfounded. I have always associated these portable stereos with fast, open cars and life on the streets. (Are they even legal in Maine's backwaters?) It was several days before I could even discuss the matter with him. Perhaps it's the prefix "boom" that makes it so difficult. I don't know.

As we sat at the kitchen table together, staring at my son's plans for his unlikely bedroom expansion and looking at an advertising flyer for a boom box with something called a "subwoofer," I could do little more than rub my chin and hope for the phone to ring. "Well?" Alyosha finally asked with a hint of impatience.

I made a lame parry with "Alyosha, you're not a teenager, you know."

He thought for a moment and then announced, "Yes, I am."

It was then I noticed that he had changed the part in his hair.

We adjourned so I could ponder these weighty events in the solitude of my private chambers.

After a long time spent staring out the window, it suddenly dawned on me: I'm not ready to have a teenager. And, at the risk of sounding trite, I'd like to add: I don't, in truth, understand them. Nevertheless, I would be a victim of circumstances in about a year's time.

Of course, I know exactly why I don't understand teenagers. Because I was not a typical teen myself. Perhaps it has something to do with having resonated to Emerson's *Self-Reliance* at the impressionable age of fourteen: when my peer group moved one way, I moved the other. On principle.

My memories of a teenagerhood of contrariness are legion. While my peers grunted through their exertions on sports teams, I whiled my time away in a basement laboratory, studying my Kenner chemistry manual with the intensity of a Talmudic scholar. While the other kids walked their dogs, I doted on my pet piranha. When long hair became the fashion, I had mine cut. I was engaged in an endless battle to define myself as anything but typical, and being called a "typical" teen was something I resisted at all costs.

And now I suddenly see my son flirting with the appurtenances of adolescence and it seems so foreign to me. It's as if someone had slipped him "the manual" in the dead of night and he's read the preamble to his own personal declaration of independence. ("When in the course of preadolescent events . . .")

As I write these words things become clearer. Tenets reassert themselves: the paradox of adolescence is that, in their efforts to become different, teenagers wind up conforming in matters of behavior and appearance.

For the four years I have had Alyosha there was only one sovereign rule: never get into an argument with a child. For there are only two possible outcomes—either I will become irrational or I will lose.

The thing is, in outlining his plans for a larger room and calmly informing me of his advanced age, my son is becoming a rational person, so now I must plumb certain pros and cons with him. But this is the really good thing about growing up: being able to explain one's thoughts and, increasingly, one's feelings. While expanding his admittedly small room is beyond our means, I may have to learn to live with a boom box, if only I can hold the thing at bay.

The other night I went to the window to check on Alyosha. He had gone outside to rollerblade. I had told him to be in by eight-thirty, and already it was nine o'clock and quite dark. But I understood completely his need to hold onto every waking moment of the waning summer. These nights of late August are rare things, real pearls in the hand, for they are so few before school comes roaring in with its obligations and deadlines.

I watched as my son skated under a streetlamp. Embedded in the silence of the night, his energy seemed boundless, his joy complete. Significantly, he had heeded my directive not to stray from in front of our home and was skating in endless circles in his pool of light.

For the moment, then, he is still locked in a snug and familiar orbit, and as surely as these nights grow cooler and shorter, I will affirm my twelve-year-old who thinks he's a teenager, despite my lack of experience. I once read it in a book, and I am reassured by its basic truth: I have never begun any important venture for which I felt adequately prepared.

AN EDUCATOR BECOMES THE EDUCATED

Helping my twelve-year-old son with his homework is often like shoveling water uphill: I soon grow weary and find myself awash in frustration.

I think it's that Alyosha has a hard time seeing me as anything other than a parent and is impatient with my attempts to play the pedagogue. And should I question one of his teachers' assignments for the sake of clarification, he's liable to shake his head in annoyance that I "just don't understand." As a result, homework can consume an entire evening, and I sometimes wonder if I'm responsible, simply because I've forgotten what it's like to be a student.

Recently, however, a change of events has thrown me into the role of being my son's student. It has to do with a knowledge he possesses and of which I am all but devoid.

Alyosha arrived from a Russian orphanage a little over four years ago. In the interim I have hired tutors—native speakers all—to assist him in retaining his mother tongue. He has not always gone to his Russian lessons with alacrity, but he recognizes the importance of not letting the language slip away. And so he has persisted in his reading, writing, and translating, developing a habit which he has come to accept as one of his routine activities.

Perhaps not realizing what I was up against, I recently decided to begin Russian lessons myself. One evening a week I walk to the home of Mrs. Markowsky, a grandmotherly woman who is a native speaker as well as a professional teacher. The first few lessons went well, and I was surprised how quickly I was able to translate the Cyrillic alphabet into useful sounds. But within a month I was mired in a language that measures grammar in pounds and uses tapeworm-length sentences to express the most succinct ideas. To hear it spoken by a native is to be witness to breathlessness.

In time I found that I was getting farther and farther behind in my homework as I struggled to acquire new vocabulary and a strange syntax. Alyosha observed my intense study sessions with a cool detachment. Every so often I'd look up at him, knowing that the knowledge I needed was tucked neatly away in his little head. And so, gathering my courage, I asked for his help.

Alyosha came right over to me and put his hand on my shoulder. "Don't worry," he said, "I'll be your teacher."

At that point I discovered a side of my son that was a revelation to me. Patiently and deliberately, he escorted me through the lessons in my primer. One of the hardest tasks was getting Russian pronunciation right. My mouth muscles were just too set in their ways, and I had a tremendous time making sounds which have no equivalent in English.

Alyosha was adept at reassuring me. "Watch me," he'd admonish with the gravity and soupçon of weariness normally associated with professors emeriti. And I'd watch as he exaggerated the sound I was after, projecting it as effortlessly as, well, as the native speaker he is. On those occasions when I still couldn't come close, he'd take hold of my face and literally mold my mouth into the correct shape. "Now say it," he'd command. With his hands still clutching my face, I'd once again attempt the desired sound, and by gum, I'd usually succeed. Of course, once released from his sculptor's grip, I'd revert to my errors of tongue, watching abashedly as my son shook his head in disappointment, the look on his face saying, "What am I going to do with you?"

What indeed. I have been under my son's tutelage for several weeks now, and despite his occasional frustration with the thick-headed student his father has turned out to be, he has stuck with me through it all. Last week he even accompanied me to my lesson with Mrs. Markowsky, like a parent visiting his child's school to verify the quality of the instruction.

During that session I was attempting to pronounce a list of words ending in what is known as the "Russian hard 'L.'" This requires one to half-swallow an imaginary potato and then speak around the obstruction. I just couldn't seem to get it, despite the pressures brought to bear by the formidable Mrs. Markowsky, master of no less than five languages. Finally, I looked to Alyosha, sitting across from me in an overstuffed chair, who urged me on with a nod of his head and a squint of his eyes. And then he spoke up. "You can do it, Dad," he encouraged.

Tapping into his confidence, I did eventually do it, and all three of us celebrated the feat with tea and pound cake. After the lesson Alyosha and I walked home together. I was experiencing a modicum of pride in my accomplishment, but beyond this I was filled with the warmth of knowing that I was not letting my son, my teacher, down.

It's not easy being a student. The task of having to constantly meet other people's deadlines and standards is daunting enough, but the drive to please the parent can rule a pupil's life.

If I can master the Russian hard "L," then I'm sure I can keep this small truth in mind.

My son and I recently came to loggerheads over a pair of shoes.

What annoyed him was the driving from store to store, the chin-rubbing as I stared doubtfully at his choices, and the head-shaking when I decided they were all too expensive, especially when one considered the rate at which a child's foot grows from month to month.

I realize now that it was all my fault. Having always earned modest salaries, I had grown extremely careful about expenses. Time and again I had proven that if one looked hard and long enough, one could come up with a perfectly serviceable pair of shoes for twenty dollars. To pay much more than that was simply frivolous. I would have made a good Puritan.

My thrift had never failed to meet Alyosha's needs. Upon his arrival from a Russian orphanage some four years ago he was a size thirteen-and-a-half. Within two months he was a one (in the arcana of children's shoe sizes), three months later a one-and-a-half, a year later a three. Through all this growth I knew exactly where to shop and when to shop there. I preferred bankrupt stores that had not yet closed, or salvage operations that bought out the stock of stores that had gone under. The result was that it was not all that difficult to find a pair of decent sneakers for six or seven dollars.

For a long time my son didn't know the difference between a no-name brand and a Nike. In the orphanage it was enough to simply have shoes. Any shoes. I recall the day I went to the orphanage to take Alyosha home. There he was, clad in torn, ill-fitting clothing, and a threadbare poplin winter coat. The orphanage had instructed me to bring clothes for him, as what he was wearing belonged to the institution.

And so I arrived with decent hand-me-downs from one of my little nephews. Under the watchful eye of his caretaker, I dressed Alyosha in jeans, hooded sweatshirt, and crisp white socks. Then I asked the caretaker where his shoes were.

"What do you mean?" she asked, her eyes widening. "Didn't you bring any?"

I explained that I didn't think I had to, not knowing his shoe size.

The woman informed me, with a hint of exasperation, that Alyosha's orphanage shoes had already been given to a new arrival.

We both stared at my son's stocking feet for a moment, the pressure of this woman's concern palpable. Suddenly, she spun about, left the room, and returned a few moments later with a pair of torn sneakers which were too small for Alyosha, but manageable. I squeezed them onto his feet and picked him up in my arms.

As we left the building and headed down the walkway I heard a wailing from behind. Turning about, still with Alyosha in my arms, I saw a little boy of about five standing in the doorway, crying his eyes out. He was barefoot. I later learned that the shoes Alyosha was wearing had been taken from this younger child. (Once back in Moscow I immediately sent them back with a pack of candy stuffed inside.)

I think it was Alyosha's experience of poverty that made it so easy to care for him during his first couple of years in the States. He never asked for anything, because he had been conditioned by orphanage life where there was very little to be had. But with increasing age (Alyosha is now twelve) came increasing sophistication, brought on, in part, by the weight of peer pressure.

Our philosophies finally clashed a couple of months ago when soccer season opened. Alyosha had told me his cleats from last year were too small. I was really proud of the bargain I had gotten on those cleats: name-brand for only $14.95. I was reluctant to believe that they no longer fit, even when Alyosha forced them on and showed me the evidence of his cramped toes.

Ah, well, if there was one pair out there for under fifteen dollars, there must be another. And so we set out along our traditional route, plying the shelves of discount and surplus stores. It wasn't so easy this time. Alyosha was now a size seven-and-a-half, one of the big boys. I couldn't believe the prices: fifty, seventy, a hundred dollars and beyond for shoes that all looked alike to me.

Alyosha's eyes, however, harbored a look of wonder. He knew brand names and styles and was able to explain to me the difference between baseball and soccer cleats. After several hours of looking, we came upon a pair for $29.95, marked down from $59.95. They had white stripes on the sides and a pattern of raised swirls behind the toes. Alyosha caressed them and turned his hopeful eyes to me.

"Thirty bucks!" I exclaimed, loud enough to turn heads. I was thinking of my $14.95 bargain of the previous year.

"Dad, it's not that expensive," my son reasoned.

I stood there, shoe in hand, rubbing my chin to a buff shine. The line between healthy thrift and parsimony is thin indeed, and I was hovering precipitously between the two. I shifted my gaze from the shoe to my son, who had launched his puppy-dog eyes at me. "I really want these, Dad," he pleaded.

I offered a nod of understanding but not acquiescence. "Alyosha," I said, quietly and clearly, "there are children in the world who don't have any shoes at all."

I was unprepared for his response. Leaning in close, my son whispered, "Dad, I know. I was one of those kids."

Totally unmanned by the power of his recollection, I could do no less than march straight to the cashier, convinced that I was a man who had found a bargain in both child and shoe.

A FATHER-SON DIALOG, WITH BALL

As if on cue, baseball gloves recently blossomed at our home in synchrony with the swelling of the buds on the silver maples. My son had dutifully excavated them from the "catch-all" basket in our unheated mudroom. The winter had stiffened the leather, and dust lay in the seams and crevices. But soon after slipping them on, we found that the fresh air and repeated poundings from fist and ball had them once again "as good as old," for there is nothing so good as an old glove.

There are few things as satisfying as tossing a baseball with one's child. My twelve-year-old has an excellent arm and a keen eye. He can throw a slider and a fastball and has an emerging curve. He's working on his knuckleball, but his hand is still too small for the trick of clamping the ball with the first joints of one's fingers.

I don't know where he gets his talent. It certainly isn't from me. I sometimes catch one of his fastballs a bit off center, and I wince as it slams against my palm. "Are you all right?" he calls with palpable concern from his end. I nod, shake off the sting, and lob the ball back.

The rhythm of the windup, the release, and the pop against leather eases me back in memory to my own boyhood. I lived in a city, and though expansive backyards were not part of my urban landscape, baseball was. Our field was the narrow, car-lined street that ran through our neighborhood. In our fervor to emulate Whitey Ford, our throws would sometimes go wild, and many a window fell prey to our enthusiasm. I can still see Mrs. Strenger, her hair up in curlers, screaming at us from the living room side of a shattered pane of glass. (Later that night there ensued deliberations among neighborhood parents, concerning who would pay for the damage.)

Unlike my son, I was a mediocre ballplayer. My father—a pitcher on an Army Air Corps team in North Africa during World War II—was dutiful in playing Sunday afternoon catch with me. I still recall his perfect pitcher's profile, which seemed to auger a blistering fastball. At the last moment, though, he'd ease off and throw me something he thought I could handle. I was a clumsy catcher who had difficulty coordinating the position of my glove with the incoming ball. But that didn't daunt my father. It was not my ability to play well that brought us out in the bright sunshine on a spring or summer day, but rather the act itself, the ritual passing of a baseball from father to son, like a legacy so important as to bear repeated emphasis.

I eventually got better at catching and throwing, to the point where I felt confident enough to go out for the seventh-grade team. It was a terrible mistake. I found myself outclassed by kids who not only had natural abilities, but had been playing on teams for years. To make a long story short, I quickly became a victim—the butt of their pranks—in an age when coaches scoffed at boys they considered "weak." I returned home defeated and mortified, swearing I'd never attempt to join a team again.

My parents noted my dejection. My mother tried to cheer me up with kind words and the promise of a special supper. To no avail. And just when I thought I never wanted to see another piece of baseball equipment, my father appeared with two gloves. "Let's go," he said, and magnetically, I followed.

We went out into the driveway and began to toss the ball, gently at first, then with a little more of what my father called "pepper." Back and forth, over and over. Every so often I heard a "Good throw" or "Attaboy." I didn't realize it then, of course, but throwing a baseball is a sort of dialog in which little is said, because little needs to be said. In the way the ball is thrown, in one's dedication to the partnership of the game of catch, one pledges one's support and encouragement and love. In this way it is an intimate act, yet one which does not crowd.

As I tossed the ball with my very capable son the other day, he expressed doubt over his ability to make this year's Little League team. Of course, I knew that he would have no problem. But stating this much would not have convinced him. Instead, it would have probably tapped into his frustration, eliciting cries of, "How do you know?" or "You just don't understand."

And so I waited for the magic of our interplay to take its effect. We threw the ball for twenty minutes—grounders, high flys, and stuff with a little pepper on it. With each successful catch my son grew brighter and more energetic. The door had opened. I hauled back and threw the ball as high as I could halfway between the two of us. We both made for it, but at the last moment we grabbed hold of each other, allowing the ball to fall with a soft thud beside us. "You have nothing to worry about," I told Alyosha as I hugged him long and hard.

He didn't say anything. He didn't have to.

Another Son's Turn at the Dance

When my thirteen-year-old son left the house for his first school dance the other night, I was filled with a mixture of awe, wonder, and nostalgia.

Just that morning, enjoying the largess of some free time, I had been cleaning out a storage room in our home. One set of shelves was filled with accumulated toys and games which Alyosha had long outgrown. Every building block, every Matchbox car, every counting game filled me with images of the little boy squatting amidst his treasures on the living room floor or making motor sounds as he raced his cars around chair legs.

I have to admit that it was with reluctance that I okayed his going to the dance. It had nothing to do with his not being old enough or responsible enough. Rather, I was hesitant to admit that, with the passage of time, Alyosha was belonging a little less to me and a bit more to the wider world.

Of course, I have mastered the old trick of easing difficult decisions by comparing my son's experiences with my own, one of which I can recall with startling clarity. I was fourteen. Eighth grade was drawing to a close, and its end would be celebrated with a graduation dance.

I duly panicked, of course. What would be demanded of me? Would I have to actually dance? I could do the Twist (this was the sixties), but beyond that—nothing. Despite my independent and hectic teenage lifestyle, in my moment of greatest need I was forced to become the little boy again and—gulp—turn to my mom.

My mother, of course, was thrilled to have me ask her for any advice at all. She immediately dropped the hi-fi needle onto an "easy-listening" LP, ushered me into the living room, and—like a combination drill sergeant and choreographer—manipulated my hands and feet into the appropriate starting positions.

I watched as she glanced heavenward for a moment, feeling for the rhythm. Then, without warning, she launched the two of us into sync with Perry Como's rendition of "It's Impossible."

Although I was supposed to be the one leading, my mom found it necessary to cart me around the living room like a sack of potatoes. Every time I flirted with despair she squeezed my hand and kept me on my feet. "Keep dancing," she'd say. "Just keep dancing. You'll get it. You're doing fine!"

It took me the longest time to learn the ridiculously simple box step. "This is good for 90 percent of the songs you'll hear," assured my mother.

Still dancing, I looked up at her with panic in my eyes. "What about the other 10 percent?" I asked.

"Don't worry," was her recurring advice. "I'll teach you to waltz, too!"

If I was middling at the foxtrot, I was a disaster at the waltz. Andy Williams's "Moon River" may have been "wider than a mile," but it was still not roomy enough for me to avoid backing into the TV, kicking over the magazine rack, and stepping on the cat. "There," she finally said, maintaining her poise against all odds.

There? There what? I felt more inept than I had before we started, because I now had proof of my terrible dancing skills. I watched with a sinking heart as my mother shut off the hi-fi and moved—no, danced—into the kitchen. She had it in her blood, and I clearly didn't. Maybe I was adopted.

Well, true to teenage behavior patterns, I frittered away a perfectly good week worrying about the dance. When the big night finally came, there were, of course, neither foxtrots nor waltzes. For the first half hour I didn't even dance. None of the boys did. We watched as a few girls dominated the floor. And then, suddenly, I was part of a crowd. Everybody seemed to be moving impulsively to some forgettable rock-and-roll lyric. I found myself facing a classmate, Barbara Chuck, and with a respectable two feet of space between us, we began to swing our arms and heave our legs asynchronously, our movements bearing no relation to the music whatsoever. If dance had changed since my mother's time, then it had simply become more democratic—anybody could do it.

I returned home that night flush with victory. My mother had waited up for me. "Well?" she asked. "Did you do okay?"

"Yeah," I said, radiating a newly acquired confidence. "I did okay." Then I went straight to bed, before she learned that the dance steps she had taught me now seemed to be extinct.

When Alyosha returned from his own school dance he was just as taciturn as I had been. "How was it?" I asked. "Okay," he said, and then skipped up to bed.

We're both still doing okay. Speaking for myself, I don't know how much of this wellness I can attribute to thrusting myself into the new frontier of the school dance. But such recollections help me to approach my son's own milestones with faith and trust. After all, he will be passing through many doors in the life that lies ahead of him, a life which will require that he—like all of us—take one step at a time.

Lightening a Load of Winter

For quite a while it seemed that winter this year would take a holiday in Maine. December was uncommonly mild, and January also came in like a lamb. But by the middle of the month it had turned cold, and a few days later twelve inches of snow fell overnight. I awoke to a neighborhood filled with the roar of snowblowers. Winter had, with a vengeance, made up for lost time.

I was one of the primitives who went out to my driveway with the low-tech device known as a shovel. So much snow! It seemed that every time I removed some from the pile, more would cascade down to replace it. And yet I went about the task with measured determination. Shoveling snow is something I like to do alone, despite the availability of my fourteen-year-old son. This isn't to say that he would ever willingly offer to help me, but he would certainly rise to the request under duress. I seldom ask, though, as I have, over the years, grown accustomed to snow removal as a solitary act.

Shoveling snow reminds me of the rhythms of haying: the sense that one is creating a useful product, in this case a clean, walkable path, through sometimes magnificent drifts, to allow the mailman through, to expedite fuel deliveries, to improve the chances of a spontaneous visit from a friend.

After I had finished the shoveling I went inside. The phone rang. It was a friend asking if Alyosha wanted to make a few dollars shoveling her walk. The offer of compensation made him very agreeable to the idea. As I drove him to the job I found myself giving him tips on shoveling, as if it were a complex art form. "Don't throw the snow in the street," I advised. Alyosha rolled his eyes. "Dad," he lamented, "why would I do that?"

I dropped my son off at the friend's house and lingered in the car for a few moments as he seized a shovel and went to work. As I watched his back I saw myself at that age, and I recalled the tremendous snowfalls of my youth. A good storm was enough to bring me to my feet at the crack of dawn, champing at the bit to get outside and make my rounds of the neighbors' houses, angling for shoveling jobs, anxious for the opportunity to make as much as five or ten dollars by suppertime.

My tool was not a fancy one: an old, heavy, rusted coal shovel with a hickory handle I think my dad had gotten from his father. I was uncommonly bold in knocking on doors at seven A.M., screaming out, "Want your walk shoveled? It's only gonna get worse!" More often than not, it was enough to secure the job for me, and I learned to enjoy the work, which I also looked upon as good exercise and a way to warm cold fingers and toes. By the end of those days, I was pretty tired. The mornings had seen me setting out with the coal shovel propped over my shoulder in a jaunty manner, but by evening I was dragging it behind me, exhausted.

After I dropped Alyosha off, I went home to some hot chocolate and a good book. It was a bitterly cold day, the thermometer hovering just above zero, with a moderate, biting wind. An hour and a half later the phone rang. It was my son. "Hey," was all he said. My reply was in kind: "Hey."

Silence.

"Do you need something, Alyosha?" I asked.

Even through the phone I could feel him shrug. "I just wanted to talk," he said and then sniffed.

Something wasn't quite right. "How's the job going, buddy?"

He finally let go. "Dad," he admitted, "I'm really cold."

"I'll be right there."

When I arrived at the neighbor's house Alyosha was standing in the driveway, wrapped around the snow shovel, his gloves off, blowing warm air through his hands. The job was a little better than half done. For a moment I considered telling him about my childhood winters with the coal shovel, but I quickly buried this impulse. He was really cold, and he clearly didn't regard snow shoveling in the poetic light I did.

"What should we do, Alyosha?" I prompted.

He looked up with those blue, wide-set eyes that never fail to stir me. "We?" he asked.

I went to my truck and grabbed my shovel. Returning to my son, I said, "Let's go," and together we put our backs into the job. In silence we worked apace, cutting a nice, clean path through the remaining drifts, making life a bit easier for somebody else, and in the process, building something to remember for ourselves.

A SON MOVES ON TO HIGH SCHOOL

My son is entering high school.

I can barely utter these words. "Entering elementary school" and "entering middle school" went down far more smoothly, but this high school business is bittersweet. Probably because it's Alyosha's last educational stop before some still vaguely-defined future. Probably because this means that, at the tender age of fourteen, my son, and his cohorts, are making their first, tentative goodbyes (though from the look of his bedroom, he is certainly unaware of this yet).

Last week there was "Family Night," a sort of introduction to the milieu of the high school and the extracurricular activities it offers. I felt distinctly out of place, as if acutely aware that I had already done the high school thing and it was somehow unnatural to be back.

After we parents and students had assembled in the gym, listening to a presentation by the faculty and members of the administration, we were released into the hallways to visit classrooms where we would be able to speak with teachers and upperclassmen about courses and activities. The rush of bodies brought back memories of hurrying to classes in the two minutes between bells, and I felt suddenly disoriented.

It occurred to me that I'd much rather be at home, or outside, or in my car—anywhere but here. And then I caught sight of Alyosha, amicably hobnobbing with his fellow presumptive freshmen, already a man about town, poised and feeling at home, possibly dreaming of his first varsity letter.

I envied him this smooth transition to high school. When I entered in the late sixties (something else I can hardly bring myself to say), the atmosphere was very different. Freshmen were the lowest rung on the ladder, and we were told not to forget it. On that very first September day, we huddled together like newly hatched chicks, our hair pomaded back and our faces buried in our collars, lest we make eye contact with an upperclassman, woe unto us!

Hazing was de rigueur. Nothing violent or injurious, but enough to add to our trepidation at being in a new environment, surrounded by so many unknowns. On my first day I recall hurrying through the hallway, holding my stack of books in front of me with both hands, clamping it with my chin. Suddenly, there was a bump, and the tower came crashing down. As I fell to my knees to gather up the books, I heard a senior laughing with his friends before moving on to his next prey.

My high school had three floors, but during that first week, freshman after freshman was sent on an "errand" to the nonexistent fourth floor ("Where the swimming pool is!") to deliver a message to the "lifeguard." We were also told that it was our job to clean up senior trays in the cafeteria and walk only on the right side of the hallways. Of course, all of this gives me a chuckle only in retrospect; at the time I felt like a leaky tugboat in a sea of freighters.

My son will not have to deal with hazing, and this is a good thing. Younger kids think the world of older kids, and as I walk my judicious ten paces behind Alyosha, I watch as upperclassmen put out their hands to him for high fives. I listen as a sophomore soccer player tells him he's happy he is joining the team. And I am encouraged when a teacher slaps my son on the back and welcomes him to the high school.

Still, I am glad to leave. As I said, I don't belong here; Alyosha does. On the way home we stop at a Dairy Queen, and halfway through my sundae I pause and look at my son, at the carefully primped hair (*sans* pomade, *avec* gel), the baggy, in-style clothes, the size-eleven sneakers, and his quiet capacity to accept things as they come. Even though he is only fourteen, I have already done almost everything I can do for him. In sending him to high school I am turning him over to other forces, to see how his convictions hold up to theirs, to see which influences resonate with him and which ones he will discount.

I may not be ready for high school, but he is. It is time.

THINGS OLD, NEW, AND TIMELESS

A couple of weeks back my fifteen-year-old son approached me with the urgent request that I take him out for "school clothes." I have to admit that I was, for a moment, at a loss for words. I hadn't heard the expression "school clothes" since I was a kid. "Alyosha," I finally offered, "you have more clothing than the crown prince of an island nation. Why don't you just wear what you have?"

Alyosha threw up his hands. "You don't understand," he said, exasperated, and gazed off into the distance.

Actually, he had it right. I'm not sure what role school clothing plays in these freewheeling days when students move from the street to the halls of academe without so much as doffing their ever-present ballcaps.

When I was in grammar school during the sixties, there was a clear delineation between school clothes and so-called play clothes. In fact, my mother had it down to a mantra. When I returned from school, she'd automatically greet me with, "Don't forget to change into your play clothes." One day, I had the temerity to dump my books on the front porch and join in a game of stickball—in my school clothes! My mom was out the door in a flash, hand on heart, pulling me out of the game with a desperation normally reserved for air raids.

For the record, my school clothing consisted of slacks—not jeans—with cuffs that were turned down year by year as I grew, a collared shirt, black oxfords, and a tie. To complete the young-scholar effect, my mother pomaded back my thick, thick hair with a tidal wave of Vitalis that hardened to a shiny, helmetlike shell.

In retrospect, it made sense. Before there were malls, video games, personal computers, and VCRs, school was just about the only show in town. More than this, school was the way out for children of working-

class families, a chance to achieve what had evaded our parents as a result of economic depression and the war that followed on its heels.

In this light, parents honored the idea of school by gussying up their
kids as a way of making them mindful that in changing from street
clothes to school clothes, they were moving from a world of play to one
of earnest hard work that would, in the end, pay off.

Things have certainly changed. When my son goes off to school in the
morning, I watch as he merges with the horde of his peers, outfitted in
tank tops, shorts, sandals, and jeans dragging beneath their heels. (Dad
to Alyosha: "But they're destroying their own clothes!" Alyosha to Dad:
"But it's the style!")

Perhaps I am hopelessly behind the times, the ant with high hopes
trying to push the rubber tree plant (I can't remember whether the little
creature succeeded or not). And yet I am haunted by a story from grammar school involving school clothes.

Most of the children I went to school with were from homes where
the nickel was tight. There was a girl in my fifth-grade class who wore
the same green sweater every day. It was growing threadbare around the
elbows, but otherwise always seemed clean and free of pills. One day, at
recess, we were playing dodgeball in the schoolyard. As Michelle ran by
me, I was, for some reason, inspired to reach out and grab her by the
hem of her sweater. The garment ripped wide open, as if it were the
thing it was time to do, and both Michelle and I froze, our mouths
agape. I could see she wanted to cry, but all I could do was offer a weak
apology. Then the bell rang.

To the credit of the child that I was, I told Michelle that I would get
her another sweater. She took this news home to her parents, but the
next day told me that they said it was okay, that I didn't have to do that.

I have told this story to my son as a way of emphasizing that there is a
difference between needs and desires, but it's so hard to get this message
across to a fifteen-year-old whose alternate address is the shopping mall.

I thought I had won the battle of the school clothes when I told
Alyosha that he should go to school in the perfectly sound, clean, well-
fitting clothes that he already had. It was at this juncture that he reminded me about the approach of his birthday. Shifting gears to that
subject, I asked him what he wanted for a gift. He turned to me and
grinned. "A sweatshirt, a pair of jeans, sneakers, and a new ballcap."

Somehow, at some level, I think I've been had.

A Son from Ukraine

The other day a friend confided to me that as a result of the World Trade Center and Pentagon catastrophes of September 11, she found herself benumbed, distracted, tired, and assigning less importance to things that had always given her pleasure. "I've always loved to cook," she reflected, "but now we simply eat out, or I cook rudimentary meals as a practical necessity."

I immediately identified with her perceptions. "Everything has been devalued," I remarked, and then I considered the ways that this has been true for me. Even taking a walk in the Maine woods in this beautiful autumn of the year has become less a means of enjoying nature than of evading recurrent media images and ubiquitous talk about the tragedy.

For me this emotional funk was, at the least, most untimely. For a year now my adoptive son, Alyosha, and I have been working toward a second adoption. Alyosha is sixteen and, like a candle waxing in intensity, has steadily warmed to the idea of having a little brother in his life. Shortly before the bombings, I received word of a five-year-old boy in Eastern Europe, and suddenly the die was cast, our common future found focus, and both of our lives inclined toward welcoming new life into our home.

And then, September 11. Everything became diminished: what to eat, what to wear, what activities to pursue on the weekend, what color roofing we should choose for our new garage. What could these things possibly matter in light of a nation's suffering? I tried to think about the adoption, but it was no-go. A much-anticipated event had become an abstraction, in a league with fretting over the vacuuming while the rubble in Manhattan was still smoldering.

In essence, in my mind I retreated from what I wanted and came to a more comforting focus on what I already had. Like the wanderer who moves closer to his campfire when the night grows dark and cold around him, I pulled closer to Alyosha. Curiously—for like most teenagers Alyosha spends a great deal of time defining independence in terms of the distance he keeps from parents—he allowed this. We ate out together, discussed the books he was reading in school, and I even snuck in a furtive hug now and then.

One night, while watching the news together, we listened to reports of the many ways people were pitching in to assist those affected by the

This essay first ran in *The Christian Science Monitor* on October 1, 2001, in the wake of the attacks on the World Trade Center.

disaster. Money, clothing, food, labor, and blood were being donated. The philosophy of the helping hand is that human charity has a habit of improving bad or unhappy situations: if you give money to the poor you make them less poor; if you give food to the hungry you sate their hunger. But what on earth can one do for the dead? Not the physical dead, mind you, but the hearts and spirits that have been deadened by events?

I looked at my son as he stared at the TV screen. "I want to do something," he said; but my mind was on the adoption which had been put on emotional, if not functional, hold. "Alyosha," I said, ever so softly, "we need to talk about this adoption. Is this something we want to do now, at this time, when we're feeling like this? It's not too late to call it off."

My son's eyebrows took flight. "Dad," he said, almost plaintively, "we *have* to do the adoption."

We have to? And then, suddenly, I caught his meaning—or the meaning I wanted to catch in his statement. Yes, we had to do the adoption. But not because we felt committed, not because we had completed the requisite paperwork, and not because we had prepared a room for the little boy. For me it was not a long stretch to assert that in the face of catastrophe, despair, and death, the antidote was life.

And so, with eyes wide open, with the support of my son, and with an energy that only hope can inspire, I will put one foot forward, and then the other. I will fly east out of New York's battered heart and return to it holding life firmly by its little hand, for it is an appropriate time to adopt, a fine season to rebuild, the perfect moment to begin anew.

ANTON AWAITS, AN OCEAN AWAY

When I adopted my son Alyosha in Russia eight years ago, in 1993, the going was anything but easy. I was a single man who found himself in a very conservative, traditional culture where I sometimes sensed that I was the object of deep suspicion. I succeeded in bringing my beautiful seven-year-old boy home, but the process had taken its emotional toll, and I forswore any future adoption gambits.

So why am I here, in Ukraine of all places, in a weatherworn village at the edge of the Black Sea, doing it again? I'm not sure I can exactly say, except that, in the intervening years since adopting Alyosha, memories of the hardships and frustrations associated with that process have ebbed, leaving a panoply of vibrant, poignant impressions that only warm me now: meeting my son for the first time, taking him by the hand and walking with him through an illuminated Red Square on a summer night, bringing him home on his first plane trip ever, and introducing him to life in Maine.

Alyosha is now sixteen, and this new boy, Anton Alexandrovich Kornilov, this small gift from the Ukrainian backwaters, is only five. How will my energetic, willful teenager react to a child who is as pliant as cotton candy? One thing I know: Alyosha longs for this little brother with all his heart. This, I think, is as good a place as any for a new relationship to start.

I sit here on the carpeted floor of this immaculate orphanage in the village of Ochakiv. Anton sits not three feet away from me, running his hand over the ball I bought for him at an outdoor market. If I do not disturb his meditation he will go on like this indefinitely. Such rhythmic activity is, I suppose, the way a child comforts himself when the present, much less the future, seems uncertain. "Antosha," I sing as I reach out and stroke his dark, close-cropped orphanage haircut. He raises his enormous brown eyes to me and smiles a curious, self-effacing smile that curls his lip over his upper teeth.

Anton's adoption had gone swimmingly until the final step: the hearing before a judge who was nothing less than hostile to my plans. "Why do you want another child?" she demanded in Russian as I stood before her with my hands folded in front of me. "You already have one."

I replied, without hesitation, through my translator, that there are only two reasons why families grow: by accident or by design. I was fortunate in belonging to the latter category: I wanted Anton in my family, and so did my son, Alyosha.

"Do you love him?" she asked in a voice tinged with suspicion.

The question caught me off guard. I felt that I knew what the judge was getting at. She wanted to know how one person can possibly love another after such brief acquaintance.

I took a breath and gave her my measured response. "Love is a process of growth," I said. "We begin with a sense that there is another person we have a good chance of growing to love. We aim for that mark and set sail for it, through rough waters and calm."

The judge did not seem impressed by my maritime allusions, despite her holding court in a town which served as a port for the Ukrainian navy. She settled back in her chair and riffled through my papers.

At this point the witnesses were heard. All were women: the head of the orphanage, the director of child welfare, Anton's caretaker. . . . One after the other they stood, drumming their hearts with their fists, pleading with the judge to approve this adoption. "I would adopt him myself," lamented the orphanage director, "but I am too poor."

In the end the judge seemed overwhelmed. "It is clear, Mr. Klose," she intoned, "that you have stolen every heart in this courtroom today." And then, lifting her eyes to me, "Including mine." Then she gave her approval to my adopting Anton. However, she imposed a thirty-day waiting period, "in case you change your mind." I told her I would not change my mind, but she stood by her decision, and I would have to return to the States for the long wait.

After my court victory I return to the orphanage. I play with Anton. We throw the ball. We put a puzzle together. He sits on my lap and kneads his fingers. I try to explain to him that I must leave for a while, but I will be back. His eyes widen and he looks up at me, frightened. Of course. He understands better than the judge what abandonment is all about, and I find myself in the unlikely role of culprit.

I take Anton by the hand, lead him to his bed, help him undress, and tuck him in. As I sit there stroking his hair he remains wide-eyed, unbelieving. Using my rudimentary Russian, I keep reminding him that I will return. I leave pictures of me, Alyosha, and our home. To reinforce this point. Then I get up to leave, looking back only once.

As I take the long, long train ride back to Kiev, through the deep, unbroken darkness of the rural Ukrainian night, I comfort myself with the realization that I will be back for Anton in a few hours less than thirty days, and that when I awake in the morning it will be only twenty-nine days. And I am mindful of something that is so true and self-evident that somebody must have written it down somewhere: when you travel well, you leave something of yourself behind.

Yes, Anton is mine now. He is part of me. But I have only temporarily left him behind, and it behooves me not to grieve our brief separation, but to look forward, with joy, to our reunion.

I am the single father of two boys—both of whom I adopted from abroad. I brought Alyosha back from Russia eight years ago, when he was seven. Anton has been here only a few weeks. A tender five-and-a-half-year-old, I brought him home from Ukraine.

It is impossible for me not to compare these two sons of Eastern Europe, which leads me to apply lessons I learned from my inaugural son, Alyosha.

I clearly recall Alyosha's first days in our home. From the beginning he slept in his own bed in his own room. However, this did not inhibit me from creeping there in the dead of night to listen for breath sounds, to watch his shallow chest rise and fall under the blanket. I had clearly assumed that the life that had been given me to nurture was as delicate as a cinder.

Anton also took to his room as if he had occupied it all his life. I put him to bed his first night with us, paged through a picture book with him, and he fell fast asleep. I retired to my own bed and slept so soundly that I almost forgot that there was an additional child in the house to care for. And I wasn't the least bit surprised when he arose in the morning, breathing on his own and looking for food.

With Alyosha, one of my concerns had been that he wouldn't make any friends. In retrospect, I am chagrined by my naïveté, but at the time I had visions of his being isolated in our house, peering forlornly out the window like a recluse. My solution was to approach parents and invite their boys over to get to know Alyosha. The result—disaster. In one instance Alyosha simply ignored the companion I had handpicked, retreated happily to his room, and I wound up playing checkers with the visiting tyke at the kitchen table until his mother came to fetch him.

I realize now, of course, that children are experts at finding playmates and developing friendships. Within very few weeks Alyosha had his own small circle of friends—each an excellent character in his own way, and all most welcome in our home.

And so I have adopted a "hands-off" policy with respect to Anton. He will, in due course, construct his own alliances. In accepting this, I feel as if a weight has been lifted from me, replaced by a sort of warm anticipation that his personal happiness will increase in proportion to the pleasure he takes in choosing his own friends.

School was a big step. Alyosha began his American educational experience in the second grade. For the first few weeks he cried almost every day, sometimes out of just one eye, a very neat trick. Of course, I was completely unmanned by this, clutching my heart and pleading, "Don't cry, Alyosha! I'll stay, I'll stay." Sometimes I even took him with me to work for fear that leaving him in school against his will would cause irreparable harm. Now that I look back, of course, I don't see an empathetic, caring parent, but rather a six-foot-three lollipop bearing the word *SUCKER*.

With Anton the situation has been completely different. As preamble to his beginning kindergarten, I brought him in for a visit. He looked around at the children, the books, the computer lab, and remarked, "So, this is my beautiful little school."

I figured this was going to be a snap. The next morning he awoke with a smile on his face, got dressed, ate a good breakfast, and we headed out for his first official school day. When I led him to the door of his classroom, however, he began to howl and sob. I dried his eyes, gave him a hug, said, "I'll be back later," and watched as his teacher ushered him into the inner sanctum. Then I went to work and had a perfectly good day. When I picked Anton up at the end of his, he looked no worse for wear. In fact, he was smiling and had drawn me a picture of a, a, well, of a something. But whatever it is, it is now taped to my office door, and I am proud of it.

The adventure goes on. It is as if Alyosha were my practice son, and Anton is the son destined to benefit from what I learned.

Of course, it is not always as simple as this. The other day I was comforting Anton after he was grief-stricken by the collapse of the traction mechanism in one of his toy cars. Alyosha was present and looked on wistfully as I hugged his little brother and assured him that, despite this catastrophe, all the stars were still aligned in their constellations. And then, on a whim, I did something that under ordinary circumstances would not be allowed of me: I went over to Alyosha and put my arm around him as well. In response, he rested his head on my shoulder.

It was only a moment's worth of affection from my teenager, but it told me that, despite all my failings, false starts, and well-intentioned parenting strategies, I must have done something right. And now, with Anton, I am being given the chance to do it right all over again.

When I brought my new son, Anton, home from a Ukrainian orphanage a scant three months ago, it was to a world where the rivers and lakes were ice-locked and the land covered in snow. Maine in winter is a thing to behold, and my home is utterly representative of the intensity with which winter exerts itself: from my backyard, down to the floodplain, and out to the Penobscot River beyond, all is a clean, white meld, a landscape united by a common blanket of snow.

What must five-year-old Anton have thought when he beheld this silent, monotonous scene, unbroken by any green, unmarred by the movement of anything except the occasional, solitary crow? Did he think he had been brought to the North Pole?

Despite the heavy snowfalls in the early part of winter, these last couple of weeks have shown a quickening of warmth. It is amazing how fast the snow disappears when the temperature rises: as I walked about my neighborhood I watched—-and listened to—water cascading from rooftops, and great, sopping pillows of snow falling from the pines and landing with broad thuds.

Anton's quick eyes resonated to the defrosting of winter as well. But he was most taken with the action in our own backyard, where the receding snow (up to midthigh not so many days ago) began to reveal evidence of things left undone at autumn's end.

Over there, by the bicycle shed, emerged a garden spade I had meant to put away after having turned my small plot at harvestime. And there, under the swamp maple, rose the white belly of my canoe, which I had hauled ashore and put to rest when the first crust of ice began to form at the water's edge.

Piles of wood, a stack of planting pots, the cellar door, a white bucket— all rising as if from sleep. As for Anton, he derived infinite pleasure from all of this. Just this morning I took him out to the wonderland and watched as he shed his winter coat (the temperature was nudging fifty degrees) and delighted in gifts revealed.

With a little help from me, he righted the canoe. Then he jumped in and ran from stem to stern, shouting, "Anton and papa! Together!" I got in, took a seat, and assured him that once the river had begun to flow again we would be out there every day. Then he leaped over the gunnels and ran to the white bucket, which he wrenched from the earth's frozen grip. From there it was on to the pots and then the woodpile. Everything was new, new. Yesterday you didn't see it, but suddenly, there it was.

Finally, Anton caught sight of my red wheelbarrow, resting up against the garden shed. It too had been cloaked in a drift of snow and ice during the winter, but now it was half-revealed, its handles protruding like the tusks of a glacier-locked mammoth. Anton took special pleasure in this, perhaps because of the color, the bright red against the bright white. He pulled at the handles, kicked the pan, but the thing wouldn't budge. He enlisted my assistance, but I couldn't move it either. He grew despondent, and I was able to draw him away from his labor only with the promise of hot chocolate.

By the next morning I had completely forgotten about the wheelbarrow. But Anton, curiously enough—for young children flit from one activity to another with abandon—had not. As soon as he was dressed he whined until I followed him outside. I watched as he pulled and kicked the wheelbarrow again, and I wondered why he was so determined to set it free. The warm night had done its work, though, so that when I laid hands upon it the wheelbarrow broke away from the ice, and there it stood, ready for ministration.

Anton immediately nudged me out of the way, took the handles in his small hands, and grunted and strained as he attempted to push the wheelbarrow through the slush. "It doesn't work in snow," I told him, but he would have none of it. It was, at the moment, the most important thing in the world for him to be able to do this. Feeling the strain of his efforts in my very marrow, I stood and observed the scene, until slowly, finally, the wheelbarrow—rusted, its tire somewhat flat, its axle bent— heeded my son's exertions and hee-hawed ahead.

It took Anton a full five minutes to push it to the other end of the yard, but once he did he threw up his hands and flashed a broad smile. For reasons unclear to my adult sensibilities, the satisfaction of his heart's desire revolved around something I thought had outlived its usefulness. I immediately recalled the poem by William Carlos Williams, which begins,

> so much depends
> upon
>
> a red wheel
> barrow . . .

So much, indeed. For Anton's mood was radiant for the rest of the day, courtesy of something that the thaw revealed.

My older son, Alyosha, age sixteen, is not a reader. When he was little I had hopes that he would be, and he certainly gave some indication of an interest in books. Once, when he was eight and we were visiting a used bookstore, he found a five-dollar bill wedged in the very first book he pulled off the shelf. The proprietor told him to keep it, and Alyosha left the store, clutching his volume to his chest, proclaiming, "I love books!"

Alas, he soon learned that books do not ordinarily contain cash money, and his interest in reading began to wane. Today he remains a lovely, decent person with a magnetic personality, but if one were to shackle a book to his leg, he would wear it until it fell apart with no thought to taking a peek inside.

This whole topic of children and books has sparked volumes of commentaries and studies. Why do some kids have a desperate hunger for reading and others feel nothing for the printed page? It has been suggested that it is a matter of parenting: if parents are readers then their children will emulate them. But I don't think it's quite this simple. As a teacher, I have had students from homes bereft of books, and some of these kids are voracious readers. Similarly, I have taught the children of college professors who approach books with the same unease and caution with which they regard poison ivy.

So why be coy? I believe that a "sense" of books is, by and large, innate, like an affinity for music or art or math. Parents can encourage the interest, but they cannot create it. I often think of the son of two of my friends. He was in the unusual position of having parents who tried to *dampen* his reading habits because they felt he read too much: at night, after lights out, he would huddle under his covers with a flashlight, reading and rereading volumes until two or three in the morning. On one occasion he read until daybreak and still was not sated.

In truth, it is a challenging age for kids and reading. There are so many competing influences, all of them visual: TV, computers, video games, movies, arcades. . . . For this reason we celebrate the child who makes books his companions, the way we cheer on the swimmer who prevails against the tide.

Until recently I had to accept the reality of my being the only reader in the house—Alyosha had cast his lot solidly with athletics (at which he excels) and the teenage social scene. And then, this past autumn, we adopted Anton. With no knowledge or feel for his likes and dislikes, talents or desires, I brought Anton home almost exclusively on the basis of his soulful eyes. But somewhere in the back of my mind I was certain that he had had little or no contact with books. I knew there had been precious few in his orphanage.

Lo and behold, his craving for books is "there." Almost from the time of his arrival Anton began to paw at the volumes on my shelves, remarking in Russian at the pictures, running his little index finger over indecipherable words. When he began kindergarten he immediately started carting books home from school (and received his first "overdue" notice a month later—I was so proud!). He will not go to sleep unless I read to him, and even after that task is done, he sits up, sometimes for one or two hours, paging, paging, paging like a proofreader.

But, like the parents of the boy under the bedcovers, do I have too much of a good thing on my hands?

Anton recently asked me to buy him a "talking" book— *Aladdin*. Throughout the text are icons (a magic lamp, Aladdin, the Sultan, a flying carpet) which relate to sound buttons on a side panel. When one encounters an icon in the text, the idea is to push the appropriate button for the tinny sound effect. This book has proved so alluring to Anton that he has asked for it every night—for two weeks now. After thirteen readings of *Aladdin*, I decided to abridge it a little. When we got to the lamp icon for the fifth time, I skipped it. Big mistake. Anton's keen ear had caught me. He insisted I go back and do it right, yelling "*Nyet*! Lamp! Lamp!"

I realized that I was now as much a prisoner of this book as the genie was of his lamp. Only there seemed to be no magic that could set me free. Alyosha must have sensed my loss of enthusiasm for *Aladdin*, for last night, as he watched me wearily pull the volume from its shelf, he interceded. "I'll read to him, Dad," he said as he took the book from my hands.

As I relaxed downstairs with one of my own titles, I paused for a moment and listened as Alyosha's reading was punctuated by Anton's pecking the sound-effect icons. Every so often both boys would laugh. This was Anton's fifteenth time through *Aladdin*, but it was the first book Alyosha had read in ages. It struck me that this could be the start of something wonderful.

Maybe there is magic after all.

"It's just like riding a bicycle" is a fixed phrase used to describe skills which, once acquired, never leave us. Think swimming, skating, or throwing a ball. And yes, think of riding a bicycle.

One does not realize how unlikely an ability this is until one has watched a child struggle and fret to master it. For me—and no doubt for everyone else who can ride a bike—it is remarkable that one has to actually *learn* to ride. I mean, it's so easy, so automatic, so innate.

Well, no, it isn't. Not in the beginning, at least. I experienced this recently when I bought a bike for my six-year-old son. He was thrilled to receive it and immediately claimed he knew how to ride, which, of course, he didn't. I watched as he insisted on trying to mount the thing on his own, and I watched as time and again the bike fell, or he fell, or they both fell. Finally Anton kicked the bike and stormed off, announcing that he didn't want a bike after all.

This, clearly, was going to be a long haul.

But nothing encourages empathy like reflecting on one's own experience. I was seven before I received my first bike. It was a gold twenty-incher. I hovered with anxious anticipation as my father carefully—and much too slowly for my needs—assembled it. Once finished, he steadied it to study the true of the wheels. Excited to the bursting point, I squeezed in between his arms and attempted to mount the bike, against my father's protests that I would need training wheels for a while.

Training wheels? Those clickety-clack appendages that little kids used? Nonsense. I would have none of it. While my father held the bike steady I placed both feet squarely on the pedals, applied pressure, and called for my father to let go.

He did, I took off, and for three or four seconds I floated like an angel—until I plowed into my mother's roses. And there I lay in a mire of thorns, petals, a few angry bees, and, of course, my bicycle.

The next thing I knew my father was bolting on the training wheels while I looked on, contrite and battle-scarred.

Anton observed me in silence as well, from his retreat behind the big silver maple in our yard, as I attached the training wheels to his own bike. Once done, the bike stood there in the driveway, glistening blue in the sun, beckoning to Anton to take a spin.

He couldn't resist, and I helped him into the saddle. I could sense his mix of unease and excitement as he sat upon his stallion, his little knuckles whitening as he gripped the handlebars. He leaned forward into the breeze, as if he were already under way.

"Give me a push," he said. I did, and I jogged to keep up as he moved off, the training wheels rattling. For a while he did pretty well, and then he attempted a turn and, training wheels or no, fell over onto the side of the road. There were no rose bushes this time, and no bees, but as I looked down at my son and tried to allay his whimpering, I realized that this was me lying there in the dirt and grit. And the look on Anton's face was the same as mine must have been those long years ago. It was the look that said, "I will never learn how to ride a bike."

I helped him up and dusted him off. "You'll do it," I consoled him. "You just have to practice." After pulling himself together, he got back on, rattled off, made another unsuccessful turn, but managed to return home with a pilot light of enthusiasm still burning.

Teaching a child to ride a bike is one of those things a parent can do with complete confidence, because a successful outcome is inevitable. At first blush it seems like an impossible challenge, calling, as it does, upon such a complex integration of the senses—sight, coordination, balance. On his first inaugural run—*avec* the hated training wheels—Anton had none of these going for him. His eyes were on the handlebars rather than the road, he couldn't pedal and turn at the same time, and he seemed perched precipitously upon his bicycle, constantly on the brink of collapse.

Then, slowly but surely, over the ensuing days it came together. The rides became smoother, the turns more competent, the falls less frequent. In fact, Anton was riding so hard that the training wheels were bending upward, barely touching the ground now. Although he wasn't aware of it (and this is the whole point), his balance had arrived.

The next morning dawned bright and warm. Anton awoke to see his bike leaning against the garage. "Where are the training wheels?" he asked.

"You don't need them," I told him. And I knew this with as much conviction as I know any great truth.

Cautiously, and with only a veneer of doubt, Anton approached the bike as I held it for him. He got on, I asked him if he was okay, he nodded, and I gave the ceremonial push. He sped off down the street with only the slightest wobble, which soon smoothed out.

When I was a boy I found a baby robin that had fallen from its nest. I kept it in a shoe box for a couple of weeks, nurtured it, and, holding it in my hand, lofted it heavenward several times a day. One day it actually flew off.

I can still remember the catch in my throat.

A SIX-YEAR-OLD SOARS ON WINGS OF LOVE

I have to admit to being taken by surprise. I had not anticipated being the father of a boy who is absolutely slaphappy in love. But here I am, trying to counsel my son Anton in the ways and wiles of humankind's most delicate dance.

Anton, by the way, is six.

Perhaps this is why I am having trouble finding my footing on this issue. I simply can't be sure what a kid so young is actually feeling. At first I thought that it would blow over like yesterday's favorite toy, but my son's sentimental trajectory has not wavered in the yearlong course of his affection for a little girl, Diana of the limpid blue eyes, who lives about a mile and a half from our home.

Whether he is making trinkets to present to her, or laboring away on a greeting card with his crayons, Anton is nothing if not constant. At one point he confided in me that he was going to marry Diana; but when I told him that it cost money to get married, he picked up the phone, called the unwitting maid, and sadly told her, "Diana, we can't get married. We need a dollar."

Ah, if only it were that simple.

Like any ongoing relationship, this one has had its valleys as well as its peaks. On one occasion Anton became teary when he saw Diana at the playground with two other children. To demonstrate his distress, he got her attention and then turned heel and stormed away, constantly looking over his shoulder to see if Diana would follow. When she didn't, he returned and scolded her. She scolded him back. The result: a two-day silence, after which they returned to being as thick as glue, the playground social machinations long forgotten.

Truth to tell, I have never seen two children play together so amicably. They share, they chat, they compromise. They are like two little stars that orbit one another out of a need for common gravity and collective warmth. I don't recall ever having to intercede to counsel kindness or break up an argument.

Of course, Anton has sometimes wanted to play with Diana at times that were inconvenient for me. Not long ago, this precipitated a rather singular event.

It was December, shortly before Christmas. The Maine winter was already well under way. I recall that late afternoon, which might just as well have been late evening because of the darkness. Anton and I had just pulled into the driveway when a light snow began to blow, the temperature lingering just below freezing. As we began to get out of the car Anton announced, "I want to go to Diana's house."

It had been a long day, and I was looking forward to a quiet evening at home, so I communicated this to my son as best I could. But his loving nature is rivaled only by his obstinacy, so he persisted. "Then I'll go myself," he said.

Now came my mistake. I decided to call his bluff. "It's a long walk," I told him, which he took as license to fly. I watched as he ran off down the street, without his coat, his arms flailing and his feet barely touching the ground. Once he gets to the corner, I thought, he'll feel the cold and the distance and turn around.

It didn't happen.

He turned the corner and left my sight. I took off after him but couldn't catch up, borne as he was on the wings of ardor. I ran back to the house and immediately called Diana's family and told them to watch for Anton, although I was convinced he'd never be able to cover the mile and a half in the dark and cold.

I got into my truck, intending to overtake him as quickly as possible. But after five minutes of driving I still hadn't spotted him.

Back and forth I drove along the stretch of road between our home and Diana's, never imagining that Anton could have gone more than a quarter mile in the short time that had elapsed. Then, extending the range of my search, I finally saw him. He was skipping—skipping!— along, absolutely radiant, like a fledgling that had flopped out of its nest and discovered, to its delight, that it could fly.

Anton had run almost a mile. I decided not to upend him right away but rather to slowly follow on the opposite side of the street. And then he stopped. At an intersection. Apparently unsure of the direction he needed to take at this juncture. But in stopping he also allowed the cold to seep in.

I pulled over, got out, and crossed over to him. He looked up at me, and tears began to well up in his eyes. "Are you mad at me?" he asked.

How could I be? Yes, he had run off, which was a dangerous and worrisome thing to do, but hadn't I given him tacit approval? Beyond this, who could quarrel with his sentiment? He had done it for love.

Bending down, I threw my coat around him and asked, "So where do you want to go now?"

"Home," was all he said.

"How about pizza first?"

His eyes lit up. "I love pizza!"

Clearly, love is a many-splendored thing, not to mention versatile.

MY SON, THE STORYTELLER

My nine-year-old son is a storyteller. Not the "Once upon a time" variety, but rather a preambler, a prose stylist, someone who consistently misses the forest because of his devotion to counting each and every tree.

Let me explain by way of example. I recently bought Anton a yellow pullover rain jacket. Two days later he came home from school without it. When I asked him where it was, he took a breath, gazed off into the distance, and began his tale: "Well, after I left the house this morning I got on the school bus and said hi to Jacob. Then it started to rain, and so we decided to play with our Pokémon cards . . ."

At this point I heaved a sigh, looked heavenward, slowly shook my head, and settled in for the long haul. After listening to the resolution of the (uneventful) bus ride, Anton's day in school, his recess in the playground, and finally the ride home, he related the story's climax: "Actually, I don't know where the jacket is."

As an admirer of both Hemingway and E. B. White, I have learned to disdain the unnecessary word. With Anton, though, I have had to accept Faulkner in my home, and I often stand in awe of my son's capacity to construct back-to-back dependent clauses while managing to bear my initial question in mind.

I don't now where his propensity for the scenic route in speech came from. I certainly didn't detect it almost four years ago when I traveled to a Ukrainian orphanage to adopt him. I distinctly recall my first impressions: Anton was tiny, wan, timid, and very, very quiet. So much so that I pointedly asked the orphanage director: "Does he ever speak?"

"Oh, yes," she assured me, "just wait."

My modest investment in patience produced a wholesale return of narrative. Once Anton got his grounding in English (he spoke only Russian at first), he seemed to draw upon it the way a hummingbird imbibes nectar. He hasn't stopped talking since.

The thing is, he really does have something to say, but there have been times of urgency when I just had to know—immediately—the answer to my question. This happened in spades one Christmas holiday when we were driving to New Jersey to visit family. A few miles before exiting the New Jersey Turnpike, Anton asked me if he could hold the toll ticket. For some reason that still mystifies me, I forked it over. "Now, don't lose it," I counseled.

As we maneuvered into a toll lane—a hair-raising experience for those who know the helter-skelter of the Jersey Turnpike—I asked Anton for the ticket. His response: "Well, the window was open, and there was a lot of traffic outside . . ."

"Anton," I said, gently, as the line of cars before me inched ahead. "The ticket. Where's the ticket?"

"Actually," he continued, "it wasn't as windy as I thought it would be. And there was this other kid in a black car who waved at me . . ."

"Anton!" I interrupted again, by now able to see the visage of the toll taker, a large, impatient-looking man. "The ticket! The ticket!"

"I had it here," he said. "But then I held it up to the crack in the window . . ."

Only one car in front of me now, as I moved into the dark maw of the toll booth. "Anton," I said, quietly and clearly. "If I don't give this man the ticket he'll charge us the maximum price. Now, where's the ticket?"

Anton's response: "What does 'maximum' mean?"

We were alongside the toll window. The man was looking at me, his palms turned upward. I turned around. "Anton, did you lose the ticket out the window?"

"No," he said. "That's what I wanted to say. I held it up, but it didn't fly out." Having said this, he calmly handed it to me.

The toll collector was still looking at me. Then he smiled as I paid my toll. "It's okay," he said. "I got a kid too."

Grateful for his understanding, I glanced back at Anton. He beamed at me, as if to say, "See, all's well that ends well."

Despite the occasional trials Anton's love of narration puts me through, I have never—except in the case of the toll ticket—sought to abridge his speech. Instead, as an outlet for all that he has to say, I encouraged him to write. He took to the art with alacrity and creates sheaves of written work so thick that he calls them his "books."

I considered that writing might take some of the wind out of his oral sails (why did I ever think this?), but it has only shored up his affection for language. The show goes on, sometimes with gratifying results: Yesterday, when he came home from school, I asked him about his day. "Well," he began, "remember how it was rainy when I got up? Actually, we could still go to recess, and . . ."

I went into my mode of half-listening restraint and was rewarded in my forbearance when, four minutes later, the plot took a wondrous turn and offered up a surprise ending. "And here," said Anton as he reached into his backpack and pulled out its contents, "is my rain jacket!"

And we lived happily ever after.

CLARINETISTRY

I am sitting in an oak windsor chair, a clarinet in one hand and a pencil in the other. Sitting next to me is my nine-year-old student, Dalton, inching his way through "Old MacDonald" with cautious abandon and the complement of squeaks and squawks expected of a beginner. He is ready at any moment to call off the effort, throw in the towel, if I but give the word. But I won't say anything which might discourage him. Instead, I begin to tap the music stand lightly with the pencil, establishing the desired rhythm and tempo. Then, finally, if he wasn't too far off, I will tell Dalton it was perfect, as I almost always do.

Nine. That's how old I was when I took up the clarinet. My instructor was an elderly, abrupt Polish man named Alexander Markiewicz, whom I called "Mr. Mac." Every Wednesday evening for a half hour I would sit in his small room above a hardware store in downtown Jersey City while he rattled the music stand with the metal band of a pencil eraser, trying to drum rhythm into my small, growing bones, shaking his head in disgust while I played. At the end of the thirty minutes I'd gaze up at him and he'd say, "Go home and do it again." Dourly. The word *perfect* wasn't in his vocabulary.

Mr. Mac hardly ever spoke to me during a lesson. When he did, he usually didn't have good things to say. The clarinet, as I had been warned, squeaked and quacked a lot, and sometimes I felt like crying because I was playing so badly. But Mr. Mac would encourage me by saying, "Don't blame it on the instrument! Keep playing!" And so I did. It sounded so awful that my lip would begin to tremble, and this quavering would pass through the reed, down the clarinet, and out the bell, where it sounded like the braying of a mule.

Sometimes Mr. Mac struck the music stand so violently with the pencil that it rocked and jiggled and I'd have to chase after it while frantically blowing my horn. Then Mr. Mac would try to sing along with me. He had a frightening voice which sounded worse than my playing. I think he knew this because he'd be singing "la-la-la" and right in the middle he'd add "and-I-can't-sing" and then go right on singing "la-la-la." When I played really poorly he'd sing, "la-la-la, sounds-like-hell, la-la-la." That's when I felt like crying again, so he'd let me stop until I had a chance to compose myself. Then I'd wipe my nose on my sleeve and go on.

One evening I was playing a little excerpt called *Piece No. 6 by Geminiani.* It was very dark outside, and a light snow was falling—a silent counterpoint which amplified my mistakes to the threshold of pain.

After I was some measures along, Mr. Mac broke in with "la-la-la" as he clanked the music stand like a cowbell, driving me deeper into the gruppettos and delicate leaps of the music, which I was butchering into something reminiscent of a hog being shackled for the slaughter. "La-la-la," croaked Mr. Mac. I couldn't go on, and perfection seemed more distant than ever.

I have not told this story to Dalton because I do not want to create the impression that he should be grateful to have a pushover for a teacher. In fact, *I* am grateful that he welcomes me back week after week. My fear is that one day he will grow tired of being lauded and will want someone capable of preaching a little clarinet fire and brimstone. I guess I could if I were so inclined, but it was Mr. Mac who ultimately taught me the value of a softer touch. You see, after I had finished blundering my way through *Piece No. 6 by Geminiani* those long years ago, Mr. Mac didn't say anything to make me feel worse than I already did. He just looked at me and smiled incredulously. "Play it again," he finally clipped with his thin turtle lips.

I wiped my hands on my jeans and began to play, slowly, as if ascending brittle stairsteps. Then Mr. Mac joined in, playing close harmony, but softly, like a shadow, letting me lead. I gained confidence, knowing that a minor mistake on my part would probably go unnoticed, buried somewhere in the two voices moving in tandem through the music. I even attempted a trill and executed it almost flawlessly. And we finished exactly together.

"You know, that was almost perfect," said Mr. Mac as he looked me over and laid his instrument across his lap.

"Almost?" I stumbled, my mouth closing quickly about the word.

"But don't worry," said Mr. Mac flatly, perhaps sensing my disappointment. "I was sixteen when I started to play the clarinet."

"Sixteen?" I echoed. And I was only nine. I had a seven-year headstart in which to purge the little piece by Geminiani of its imperfections. Seven years. An eternity.

Mr. Mac turned the page of my music book and began to teach me something completely new. But my eyes wandered over to the dark window as his voice rasped and sputtered in the background, growing more and more distant as I watched a soft pillow of fresh snow gather and grow on the ledge. It was white beyond belief. Untouched. Perfect.

Nine-year-olds are sometimes too fragile to be told anything less.

The other day I was visiting a friend whose daughter, at age fifteen, had become a committed clarinetist. In a couple of weeks Katya would try out for "All-State"—Maine's handpicked coterie of serious young musicians. Her apprehension was palpable. And with good reason: her audition piece was a passage from Mozart's *Clarinet Concerto*—a virtuoso work.

Katya's situation immediately reminded me of my own public debut many years ago, when I was a budding clarinetist.

At the age of nine, I was already squeaking and quacking my way through private lessons with my teacher, Mr. Mac. I sensed that he liked me, even though he sometimes held his head in his hands and moaned as I played. In any case, by the time I was ten he thought me accomplished enough to participate in a young musicians recital, as third clarinet in a trio playing "Santa Lucia." Though initially flattered by Mr. Mac's faith in my abilities, I was soon unnerved at the prospect of playing before an audience. I left his studio that evening filled with dread.

Even as a child musician I recognized that performing on stage must be a very demanding thing. It wasn't like reading a composition in front of a class, where one could stumble, clear one's throat, say "Now where was I?" and press on. Rather, playing music in public was unforgiving and left no room for error but plenty for humiliation.

I went home and attacked "Santa Lucia" with verve and determination. The piece wasn't technically difficult, but I had trouble with its lovely, cascading slurs. Every time I tried to lend them some soul, I envisioned the pained expression of Mr. Mac, rocking his head in his hands and groaning, "Awful, awful, awful." To soothe my apprehensions I'd close my eyes and retreat to the only piece I knew by heart—"Rambling Rose," whose simple, protracted quarter and whole notes I could play flawlessly.

Incredibly, I didn't meet the other two young clarinetists I was to play with until the afternoon of the recital. Mr. Mac gathered me and the Serafino brothers together backstage and gave us the most cursory of advice: "If you make a mistake, keep playing!" And with this he retreated to his seat in the audience, next to my parents, whose faces were aglow with pride and anticipation.

We three clarinetists did little more than hover in the wings and stare at each other while the recital powered up. Our trio was preceded by a lanky high school senior playing jazz breaks on a baritone sax as big as my bike, and a boy named Butch who hammered out a ferocious—and lengthy—drum solo. I was encouraged when I looked out at the audience and saw Mr. Mac holding his head: perhaps this meant that no matter how poorly I played, he would look upon it as respite from Butch's relentless banging.

After Butch had removed his hardware, the recital director walked onto the stage and introduced our trio. The three of us—in suit jackets, ties, and pomaded hair—filed out with clarinets in hand. We stood before our cardboard stands and arranged our music. The first clarinet, Anthony Serafino, sounded an "A," and the second clarinet and I followed suit. I have no idea whether we were in tune or not; it just seemed like the thing to do.

Without warning, Anthony intoned "Santa Maria," taking me by surprise. I immediately fell two measures behind but caught up by converting a *moderato* to a *vivace*. I had never played as part of an ensemble before and was amazed at the extent to which an individual instrument's voice was buried in the collective noise. I soon felt confident enough to lift my eyes from the music to survey Mr. Mac. He was sitting stock still, wincing slightly, but otherwise bearing up under our tooting.

I turned my eyes back to the music and—oh-oh. Gone. I mean, the music was still there, but I had lost my place. I glanced up at Mr. Mac, who was now leaning forward in his seat, as if straining to will the notes to me by telepathy. Sweat gathered in my palms and my heart began to race. What to do? Well, I did what I had always done in a musical tight spot: I closed my eyes and began to play "Rambling Rose," in the hope that no one would notice.

Amazingly, I finished at just about the same time as the Serafino brothers, with only a measure or two to spare. The audience broke into reserved applause (except for my parents, who were on their feet, clapping wildly). Mr. Mac, for his part, was simply staring incredulously at me, shaking his head in disbelief. Needless to say, that was my first and last public performance. I was never asked to audition for anything as lofty as All-State.

I didn't tell this story to Katya, of course. She was already nervous beyond consolation. But she did ask if I had ever played in public.

"Oh, yes," I told her. "When I was only ten years old."

"Did you make any mistakes?" she asked.

"I played 'Rambling Rose' flawlessly," I assured her. And, having told the truth, I turned the conversation to the impending winter and our collective hopes for the New Year.

MY SON, THE CLARINET, AND ME

One of my sublime pleasures is to steal a half hour or so to play my clarinet. Especially on these bitter winter nights, when even the furnace doesn't seem quite enough to warm the walls. Music heightens my metabolism to the threshold of comfort.

My nine-year-old son, Alyosha, has developed an appreciation for the clarinet as well. For a year now he has been in the habit of sitting cross-legged at my feet while I play, rocking to the music, and then, without warning, bursting into song. At first I was startled by this, but I have long since learned to maintain my composure in the face of his assault. There is a certain sense of loss, of course, because Mozart for solo clarinet is sweet, but when accompanied by a nine-year-old boy howling nonsense lyrics the leap from classical to cacophony is almost too much to bear.

I've never tried to discourage Alyosha from accompanying me, because although the effect is enough to drive the cows from home, the *idea* has irresistible appeal: rondo for clarinet and voice performed by father and son. All of this led me to wonder what kind of musical aptitude Alyosha might have. No sooner had this thought occurred to me than a calling card crossed my path. A new violin teacher had moved to the area. From Russia yet. The real thing. He was looking for students. I approached Alyosha and asked if he'd like to take music lessons. He nodded eagerly. But when I suggested strings he only frowned. "Clarinet," was his reply.

The problem is, the clarinet is a notoriously difficult instrument for a young child to learn. It therefore baffles me that clarinets, more than any other instrument perhaps, are thrust into the hands of aspiring grammar-school musicians who are then commanded to play like angels. I still don't understand how their music teachers are able to survive the nerve-racking squeaks and squawks and quackings of a legion of clarinets in beginners' hands. The violin seems so much more accessible: anyone can pass a bow across a string and get at least a semblance of a note. But it might be a week or more before a child can get a clarinet's mouthpiece to behave properly and generate one modest, plaintive tone. Perhaps this is why the nation is littered with a legacy of clarinets in the dark recesses of hall closets.

I explained all this to Alyosha. The heaviness of the instrument, the fragility of reeds, the difficulty of producing a clear tone, saliva dripping out of the bell and onto one's shoe. His response was to ask if he could try my clarinet. It was an inspired thought! Now he would see for himself how frustrating an affair it was. I handed over my professional LeBlanc Paris instrument, helped him align his fingers and hold the clarinet correctly, watched as he took a deep breath, and—darn if he didn't get a proper "G" out of the thing! But subsequent efforts were less productive, and he retreated to kneeling at my feet, howling as I intoned a Mozart divertimento. After a few bars he broke in with, "Is it hard, Dad?" I paused and reassured him that yes, it was very difficult and wouldn't he rather play the violin? A broad smile broke across his face as he shook his head. "Clarinet," he said, slowly and with deliberation, as if he were tasting the word.

A big break for my point of view came a few days later when a flyer went out from our local arts center that the violinist Itzhak Perlman would be giving a concert. It was time to bring out the big guns. Without hesitation I picked up the phone and ordered two tickets. In the meantime I obtained a video, *Perlman in Russia,* about the violinist's triumphal debut in that country with the Israel Philharmonic. Alyosha and I cuddled on the couch and watched the spectacular production, the masterful playing of Perlman providing a background thread as various aspects of Russian culture were highlighted. Alyosha, to my delight, was captivated. He clapped avidly at the end of every piece. "How does he do it?" he asked. "Practice," I said, nodding sagely. "Practice." And then, "Would you like to learn to play like that?" Alyosha reflected for only a moment. "Nah," he said. "Clarinet."

The crusade to acquaint my son with strings had taken possession of me. Like a character in a Poe story, I was becoming single-minded about the idea. A few days later we found ourselves in a packed concert hall, leaning against the balcony railing, awaiting the appearance of the master violinist. Alyosha was one of the very few children in the audience. When Perlman appeared my son's hands fluttered like a flight of doves. And then the music began. Slow pieces, sweet pieces, playful pieces. The coup de grâce was a devilishly difficult, fast piece called *Dance of the*

Goblins by Bazzini, which caused Alyosha to spring from his seat with wild-eyed enthusiasm. "How does he do it?" he pleaded. "*How?*"

It was late when we returned home. As I tucked my son into bed I asked him if he had enjoyed the concert. "He was great," he said. "No, he's the greatest."

It was time to strike. "So, now would you like to learn the violin?" I asked, flush with anticipation. Alyosha looked at me with disappointment, as if I had still not gotten the message. "Dad," he said, "he's the greatest with the violin, but he can't play the clarinet as well as you."

I was totally unmanned by my son's estimation of my abilities. But it went beyond this. Alyosha's sentiment had nothing to do with music and everything to do with me. The magnanimity of his statement was one of those singular gifts of son to father, and it never fails to warm me, even when the outside thermometer dips off the scale. I immediately dropped any plans for negotiating Alyosha into the world of the violin. And so, as I save my pennies for his first clarinet, he continues to sit at my feet, assigning lyrics to my imperfect renderings of Mozart's beautiful melodies. And in those moments when the accompaniment begins to weigh heavily upon me, I am encouraged by my son's expression of faith—that I am a better clarinetist than Itzhak Perlman.

Once again, anything is possible, and together we move into the minuet.

THE CANTANKEROUS CLARINET CALLS

When I was nine I started taking clarinet lessons. For six years I persisted, my teacher watching and listening as I played my little excerpts, his face contorted in pain as my instrument squeaked, squawked, and hissed. Sometimes I think he tolerated me as a student only because he felt so good when I finally stopped playing.

Such is my lingering impression of childhood music lessons. Playing the clarinet was—and continues to be—a special challenge. The instrument is a mechanical nightmare topped by a notoriously uncooperative sliver of wood called a reed.

I therefore made every effort to usher my young son in the direction of strings, navigating a treacherous course between his alternately voiced desires for woodwinds and drums. But in my son's ardor to emulate his good old dad, Alyosha settled on the clarinet.

I found a used clarinet in a local advertiser. It had been played and abandoned by a boy apparently wiser than my son, one who recognized the limits of his own endurance in the face of an instrument that has a tendency to go its own way despite the musician's best efforts.

When I brought the clarinet home Alyosha fell upon it with hunger in his eyes. Slowly, meticulously, and with monumental patience, I attempted to show him how to put the instrument together and how to care for it while he tried to insert his mitts between mine in a frenzy of enthusiasm. As I spoke he kept interjecting, "I know! I know!" To which I replied, "How do you know? How *could* you know?" I stopped just short of losing my patience and realized that of all the possible clarinet teachers for my son, I would be the worst.

I suggested to Alyosha that he take lessons with someone else, someone he would know only as a teacher and not a parent or friend. He wouldn't hear of it and was convinced of the logic of his reasoning: why should we pay a teacher when dad could do the job for free?

The first couple of days went rather well. I gave Alyosha his initial lesson, and he listened attentively and then tried his best to play the music. By the third day, however, he began to show impatience with having to repeat a phrase until he had it licked. His approach to music was much like his approach to soccer: Get to the goal! The goal! His measure of a lesson well done was a function of how much—and not how well—he had played.

In time I found myself approaching those lessons with something resembling trepidation, realizing that Alyosha had become as frustrated with me as I was with him. I really couldn't be his teacher in any productive way: he knew my weaknesses and everything in my bag of disciplinary tricks. If he was uncooperative, what could I do? Threaten to send a note home to his parents?

Effective teachers don't let their pupils know too much about them. They seldom raise their voices and rarely drop the second shoe. In this way teachers are somewhat of a mystery to their students. It's the little unknowns that make the relationship between them and their pupils such a charged one and generally give teachers the control they need to get things done in the classroom.

The other night I was engaged in yet another lesson with Alyosha. He was playing quite well, making commendable progress. Then I introduced a new concept—the dotted half note—and he kept missing the count. So I kept insisting that he repeat the exercise. He resisted by refusing to do so and instead played through to the end (Goal!).

"Alyosha," I said, "you missed the count."

With hurt in his eyes and grit in his voice, he told me, "You're not my teacher." And then he braced himself for my reaction.

Curiously, I was not in the least offended. Because he was right. Well, sort of. I was teaching him but not very effectively. I offered to resign as clarinet teacher de luxe. But Alyosha rejected this. For both our sakes, though, I decided to limit the formal lessons to once a week. In the interim Alyosha would have to practice on his own.

And then, last night, when I thought my son had gone to bed, I suddenly heard the plangent tones of his clarinet emanating from the library upstairs. I put down my book and listened. He was attacking "Ode to Joy" over and over, but darn if he wasn't counting those dotted half notes wrong, still shorting them a beat. In my head I kept pulling for that extra beat, just once, to satisfy my need to hear the piece played correctly. But despite the most incredible compulsion to speak out, I stopped short of uttering a syllable and allowed Alyosha, at long last, to find his own way in the music.

Isn't that what any good teacher would do?

SUDDENLY, I WAS IN A POLKA BAND

I am not a clarinetist by profession, but I don't think I love the instrument any less than the most accomplished virtuoso. Fortunately, one does not have to be a consummate artist to experience the rewards of making music.

I have a friend who is a pianist, and once a week we meet in his living room, where we hack away at sonatas with the abandon of true believers. At the moment we are creeping through the deeply romantic second sonata for clarinet and piano by Brahms. It is an incomparable piece, in a league of its own, all the more so when one considers that Brahms wrote it almost as an afterthought, at a time when he had officially retired from composition.

Rick and I have been delicately managing this piece for several weeks now, observing the composer's every gloss with the devotion of the orthodox. This careful attention to detail makes me smile when I recall an early stint as a member of an ensemble, when details would have only gotten in the way of playing music.

I was only thirteen and had been playing the clarinet for four years, taking lessons from Mr. Mac. I don't think he had a high estimation of my clarinetistry, as evidenced by his wincing and moaning as I stumbled through the lessons. I was surprised, then, when one day he invited me to play in a polka band to which he belonged. "Really?" I remember asking, deeply flattered.

"I'll pick you up Friday at seven," was all he said.

A band. Gee. Maybe I was doing okay after all.

That Friday evening I found myself sitting obediently in the dim basement of a Mr. Bernie Nieziewicz, my clarinet clutched at the ready. Mr. Nieziewicz was the band's drummer. There was also Mr. Godlewski on accordion, and of course Mr. Mac, and now me.

"Okay, kid," Mr. Nieziewicz said without so much as a *How do you do?* "The Cherry Pickers."

Like a freight train with a schedule to meet, the band immediately pumped up without me, and I hustled to catch up, wetting my reed and slapping my way through the sheets of music Mr. Mac had set in front of me. I finally found my place and jumped, or rather stumbled, in.

The music was relentless—an incessant "One-two-one-two / bam! bam! bam! bam!" paced by Mr. Nieziewicz's furious drumming. All of us played along with no modulation whatsoever. Every so often I'd sneak a peek at Mr. Godlewski squeezing the life out of his accordion and Mr. Mac puffing away red-faced at his clarinet. One of my fears had been that I'd make mistakes, embarrassing Mr. Mac. But two minutes into "The Cherry Pickers" I realized that I had little to worry about, as I was simply part of the cacophony.

The pieces that followed "The Cherry Pickers" adhered to the same routine: we always played right through to the end, no matter what, despite quacking sounds from the clarinets and missteps from the accordion. Then the music would stop, we would look at each other in a self-congratulatory way, and go on to the next number.

"Okay," said Mr. Nieziewicz after we had done a few polkas. "Now for an oberek. Let's do 'Turn Slowly.' "

An oberek is tamer than a polka. It's a slavic dance in respectable 3/8 time instead of the desperate, winner-take-all 2/4 of the polka. But no matter, we banged the oberek into submission anyway, with Mr. Godlewski calling out halfway through the piece for, of all things, more drums. Mr. Nieziewicz was happy to comply, until the oberek sounded more like, well, a polka.

That night we made our way through pieces which such names as "Klara," "Sucha," "Coney Island Polka," "Papuga Polka," and "Hot Kielbasy Polka." This last one had lyrics. On the repeat Mr. Nieziewicz and Mr. Godlewski suddenly groaned out, "You can have Liz Taylor and your pretty Lola / You can have Jack Benny's do re mi fa so la / You can have your corned beef and your hot pastrami / But give me, give me, that good ol' hot kielbasy!"

After the practice, while the music was still ringing in my ears, Mr. Nieziewicz looked over at me and said, "You're pretty good, kid, you know?"

Despite this auspicious beginning, and Mr. Nieziewicz's kind words, the band never played again. When I asked Mr. Mac about it, he just shrugged and said, "Not enough gigs." And then, turning his narrow, wide-set eyes upon me, he asked, "You did have fun though, didn't you?"

Yeah, I had fun. And that, for me, was the whole ball of wax. Now that I am playing Brahms, I don't consider myself to have advanced in any way or to be playing a "higher" form of music. For even when Brahms is at his sweetest and most emotive, I can still recall the ringing harmony and bouncy rhythm of "The Cherry Pickers" with a warmth that one of the master's sonatas is hard-pressed to evoke.

For someone like me who is far less than a virtuoso, people really do make the music.

A Traitor Clarinet in the Ranks

When I was an exchange student in Germany, I had the opportunity to play clarinet in a community orchestra.

Music is the lifeblood of Germany. In the land of Beethoven and Brahms it is more democratic than politics, as there seems to be room for anybody with a horn to toot or a fiddle to pluck. I never lacked for an opportunity to play with other students—almost none of whom were music majors. It is as natural for a German to play an instrument as it is for an Indian to speak more than his local dialect. There were times when I played every evening of the week. Clarinet in hand, I would go from door to door, itinerantly, availing myself of duets, trios, and quartets. When no clarinet part was called for, I simply transposed the viola part, happy to be there.

While chamber music is an exercise in egalitarianism and partnership, where everyone gets a chance to shine as well as support the efforts of one's fellow players, the orchestra offers one a chance to be part of something much bigger. But foreign clarinetists have a peculiar problem playing in German orchestras: most clarinets in the world feature an arrangement of keys called the Boehm system, developed in the 1840s in France. Germany, however, went its own way with the Oehler system. The two clarinets—French and German—really do look different. They also sound a bit different, the German clarinet to most ears being "darker," and the French clarinet "brighter." The Germans are orthodox about this difference. Ads for clarinetists in German newspapers often carry the caveat: *KEIN BOEHM!*

Undeterred, I answered a call for a first-chair clarinet in one of Göttingen's orchestras. As it turned out, I was the only clarinetist who showed up. Without so much as greeting me, the conductor, Herr Weiske, a corpulent, bearded, imposing man in his early forties, gestured with his baton toward a vacant seat in the rear. He had no reason to assume I wasn't German, and even less reason to suspect that I had just smuggled a Boehm clarinet into his orchestra.

The second-chair clarinetist, a young man studying at the university, nodded toward me and smiled his greeting. When he saw my clarinet, though, his eyebrows flew up. "This should be interesting!" he said.

The conductor raised his baton, hardened his eyes, and we began to play the first movement of Beethoven's Eighth Symphony, which contains a clarinet solo in the third measure. After the full ensemble thundered its introduction, I tweedled my brief passage against the backdrop of an absolutely silent orchestra, which then returned full force to echo my solo.

Herr Weiske beat his music stand with the baton. "*Nein! Nein!*" he barked. "*Etwas stimmt nicht!*" (Something is wrong!)

The problem was one that I had forgotten about: German clarinets are pitched a fraction higher than French ones. I was flat, but perhaps the conductor simply thought he was hearing things. He raised his baton, shook his head and shoulders as if to dispel a chill, and roused us into the Beethoven again. The orchestra roared and I tweedled, this time biting down on the reed—a maneuver to raise the clarinet's pitch.

No. Herr Weiske beat his podium viciously, raising a whirlwind which sent his pages to the floor. This time he had me in his sights. He pointed the baton at me and looked down its length, as if he were aiming a weapon. The other players turned and fixed their gazes on me. Herr Weiske spoke: "Clarinetist," he said, "do we have a problem?"

I suddenly felt like a nine-year-old caught with his hand in the cookie jar. I was surrounded. Strings to my left and woodwinds to my right. There was no way out. The conductor repeated his question. "Do we have a problem, clarinetist?"

I struck a serious expression. "*Ja, Herr* Weiske," I said. "I think the orchestra is sharp."

Herr Weiske shook out his whole body like an old blanket. That unwelcome chill had returned. He rapped the podium again, but the entire orchestra had fallen into animated discussion. He signaled me to approach him, with my instrument. I dutifully slinked through the forest of bassoons, French horns, and cellos. When the conductor saw my clarinet he was bug-eyed. He reached out to touch it but quickly retrieved his hand, as if fearing contamination. A flutter of monosyllables erupted in the orchestra. ("Boehm!" "Boehm!" "Boehm!")

A thousand thoughts ran through my mind as I stood in Herr Weiske's ample shadow, the players at my back murmuring "Boehm!" like a Greek chorus. Was this the first time the sainted Beethoven had been intoned on German soil with a French clarinet? Would the conductor break my instrument over his knee? Would I be tossed out with a simple rebuke, or was there a specific punishment reserved for smugglers of Boehm clarinets?

As it turned out, the calendar was my only ally. The concert was in three days—not time enough to find another clarinetist of the proper stripe and key arrangement. Herr Weiske told the second- chair clarinet to switch places with me, but he shook his head, declining the limelight. The bottom of the barrel had already been scraped, and I was it!

The conductor looked at me. "Can you squeeze that reed a little harder?" he asked. "I'll try," I said contritely, and for the rest of that evening and during the following rehearsals I bore down on my reed until I was examining my lip for splinters.

On the night of the concert, in an old landmark church in the heart of Göttingen, Herr Weiske looked particularly edgy. When he mounted his podium and glanced my way I realized that it was because of me. He still wasn't satisfied with my pitch. But there was a full house of expectant Germans, so what could we do other than play on?

The oboeist rose to intone his "A," to which an orchestra traditionally tunes. But then a strange—and unprecedented—thing happened. The conductor motioned to him to resume his seat.

The oboeist looked about himself, incredulously, convinced that Herr Weiske was pointing to somebody else with his baton. But he gestured more vigorously to the oboeist, and the message was clear: SIT DOWN!

Then Herr Weiske turned to me, motioning me to my feet. I rose, with the eyes of my fellow players upon me, wondering what was going on. Herr Weiske called me forward, and I stumbled through the orchestra, clarinet in hand. The conductor rapped on his podium. The orchestra fell silent, as did the audience. "Play your 'A,'" he said. I pointed to myself and threw him a questioning look. "Me?" I asked. Herr Weiske nodded.

And so I inhaled deeply, slipped the mouthpiece between my lips, and expressed the most soulful "A" I could muster. Herr Weiske signaled to the orchestra, and each and every member busily tuned down until their pitch was even with mine. I have said this often, and it has thus far gone uncontested: I believe this was the first, and perhaps only, instance of a German orchestra ever tuning down to accommodate a Boehm clarinet—an ugly duckling—in its ranks.

We played the Beethoven, my clarinet sang, and I distinctly recall that an elderly woman in the first row of the audience dabbed a tear from her eye.

Even in a land of musical orthodoxy, it is possible to bend a little, or a lot, and still give Beethoven his due.

MY FINE-FEATHERED ACCOMPANIST

Two years ago I gave in to my son's request for a parakeet. While I was cool to the idea at first (anticipating that care of the pet would eventually fall to me), I immediately took to the young bird with plumage reminiscent of clouds passing against the bluest of skies.

My son, for his part, envisioned his new pet sitting loyally on his shoulder and carrying on a running dialogue. Alyosha and I commenced the language instruction without delay, talking to the bird at every opportunity, repeating stock phrases like "Pretty boy," "Good bird," and "Hello! Hello!" But all he would do in return was whistle or chirp or peep. This inspired my son to christen his new pet "Harpo." And true to his namesake, he has never spoken a word.

But, as if to compensate for his lack of verbal skills, Harpo is highly animated, a veritable acrobat both within and outside his spacious cage. The variety of his vocal emanations has also increased. There is the roosterlike screech at dawn, his cooing whistle of contentment once the day is under way, the whoop that constitutes his call for attention, and—perhaps most satisfying—his response to music in the form of a panoply of squeals, pips and squeaks.

I first became aware of Harpo's musical aptitude when, one day, I was practicing the adagio to Mozart's magnificent *Clarinet Concerto*. As I piped my horn as passionately as the acoustics of our small library/den area would allow, I became faintly aware of a change in Harpo's vocalizations. At the beginning of my practice he had been cooing amicably in his cage, but several bars into the adagio he seemed to be modulating his tones and marking time. It was very pleasant, and I suddenly realized why classical composers such as Boccherini had written pieces incorporating birdsong.

I immediately called Alyosha's attention to his pet's songfulness, but he paid it only passing mind, as it didn't involve rock and roll. As for me, I was fascinated by Harpo's taste in human music. Little did I suspect at the time, however, the interesting turn his preference would take.

It wasn't long before I came to look forward to my impromptu duets with Harpo, even though he seemed unable to discriminate between composers. Mozart, Beethoven, and Bach—they were all the same to him and elicited the same sweet tones again and again. But one evening my mood called for something different, and without giving a thought to Harpo, I broke into a rolling Scott Joplin rag called *The Cascades*. Within a few bars I was aware of something different in the air. It was Harpo. He had suddenly shifted gears, there was a new flutter in his voice and, to put it in the vernacular, he seemed to be "groovin.'"

I stopped playing for a moment, got up, and went over to the cage, where Harpo had fallen silent. He looked up at me, puffed out his feathers, and then preened. I stepped back and intoned the opening bars to

Mozart's *Clarinet Quintet.* Harpo responded with a series of peeps. I switched to Haydn's *Emperor Quartet,* and Harpo continued to peep, throwing in an occasional squeal for interest. Then, without warning, I hit Joplin's sweet and lively rag *Leola* ("Respectfully dedicated," in one of Joplin's trademark annotations, "to Miss Minnie Wade"). Harpo immediately puffed out his feathers, shook his head, and let go with a potpourri of peeps, cheeps, and whistles.

And so it went through the evening. I played as many rags as my embouchure could sustain: *Peacherine Rag, A Breeze from Alabama, Palm Leaf Rag, Eugenia,* and the lovely *Bethena* ("A Concert Waltz—Respectfully Dedicated to Mr. & Mrs. Dan E. Davenport of St. Louis, Mo."). Harpo sang along without letup, each rag seemingly a fresh invigoration.

As for Alyosha, he would still rather have a bird that's a chatterer instead of a hepcat. But I think he appreciates the singular talent of his much-loved pet, who can tell the difference between a minuet and a syncopated ragtime march.

Now that spring is coming on I look forward to being able to throw open the windows on warm evenings so that my neighbors can share in our avian largess as well. In the meantime, I continue to practice away, with Harpo as my tireless accompanist (or perhaps it is I who accompanies him?). I still can't get over it. Ragtime. He really likes ragtime. But then again, who doesn't?

NOSTALGIA

When I was fifteen I read a story in a *National Geographic* magazine about Teddy Roosevelt. It related how, while Roosevelt was crossing the Amazon River on one of his expeditions, a piranha had bitten off a piece of his heel.

Why this incident should have inspired me in any way I can't say, but by the time I had put the magazine down I had decided that I desperately wanted a piranha.

I bought a floppy little how-to book for seventy-five cents titled—what else?—*Piranhas.* On the cover was a spectacular, iridescent specimen with its lower rack of teeth bared. The book contained descriptions of about ten species, some of which were vegetarians. Having a vegetarian piranha would certainly have made feeding no problem, but somehow it defeated the idea of what the fish is all about. It would have taken the thrill out of keeping one, kind of like having a knife that couldn't be sharpened.

I finally came to a photo of a steel-blue, deep-bodied fish with a red belly. Its teeth were fully bared in an ominous smile. The caption read, "*Serrasalmus nattererei,* the red piranha. This is the most dangerous species. Inexpensive, though, and easy to keep."

This is the most dangerous species. Well then, why would I want any other? I already had an aquarium, so I asked my parents if I could buy a fish for it. "Of course," they said.

I cracked my piggy bank, got on the city bus, and rode down to Sal's World of Pets, where the owner, an ex-boxer, did a brisk business in exotic fishes.

Sal had a tremendous number of aquaria, all clean and well-kept—in contrast to Sal himself, who wore a threadbare undershirt and smoked cheroots. But he knew his fishes. I asked him where he kept the piranhas and he laughed—a low, mischievous chortle. "They're way in the back, kid," he said, waving me toward the rear of the store. "You'll know 'em when you see 'em."

I passed down a long aisle bordered on both sides by bubbling, glowing aquaria containing, for the most part, tiny, colorful tropical fishes. Against the rear wall, though, were a number of tanks bearing stickers with skulls and crossbones. The piranhas! I was a little disappointed with the first ones I looked at. They seemed pretty innocuous, small-mouthed and timid looking, content to be in Sal's care.

And then I saw it—about the size of a toddler's hand, hovering in the middle of a ten-gallon tank all by itself, bathed in a soft fluorescent light which set its colors, its translucent fins, and yes, its teeth off to wonderful effect—*Serrasalmus nattererei,* the red piranha. *The most dangerous species.*

"You want that one, kid?"

It was Sal, who had crept up on me. "That's Joe, and he's a beauty," he continued. "And only eight ninety-five."

I reached into my pocket and pulled out a crumpled wad of bills and some change. "But I've only got six dollars and fifty cents," I mourned.

"Like I said," smiled Sal with the cheroot wedged in the corner of his mouth. "A bargain at six fifty."

I watched as Sal lifted the plexiglas lid from the tank and inserted a net on a wire handle. The piranha went into a frenzy, charging and tearing at the net, swimming in mad circles, splashing water in Sal's face, extinguishing his cigar. "I'll tell ya', kid," he said without taking his eyes from his work, "you're gettin' a lot of fish for six bucks. This is the same species that bit Teddy Roosevelt's foot off."

Sal eventually succeeded in scooping Joe out of the tank. He put him into triple plastic bags with some of his native water. Then he took a length of jute and tied an immense knot in the top, put the plastic bags inside a paper bag, took my money, and handed the piranha over to me. "Want some advice, kid?" he asked.

I nodded anxiously.

"Run!"

I could hear Sal laughing as I tore out of the store. I ran to the corner and shuffled about nervously as I waited for the bus. When it finally arrived and opened its doors I scrambled aboard. But the driver threw me off because I had spent all my money on the piranha. So I had to run home. I could feel Joe ramming and tearing at the bags along the way. What would I do if he managed to break through?

By the time I got home, Joe had ripped through the two inner bags, and only the third stood between life and dessication in the gutter. But I did it. I got him into the ten-gallon tank I had set up the night before. All it had in it was a rock, which Joe immediately sought out for cover. I turned on the fluorescent light and looked at him from the side of the tank, hovering there behind his rock. He was beautiful, with a cool deliberation in his eye that told me this was, indeed, a dangerous fish. I had gotten him home safely. The next hurdle was my parents.

When my father saw Joe he bent down in front of the aquarium and looked askance at the partially obscured piranha, pulsing behind its rock. And then his eyebrows rose. "Hey, waaiiit a minute," he said. "This fish has teeth!"

"It's a piranha, Dad," I announced with sublime joy.

"You're kidding," he said. "Didn't a piranha bite off Teddy Roosevelt's leg?"

"What does he eat?" asked my mother, standing at a safe distance, her hands clasped in front of her.

"Anything with blood in it," I said proudly. "Preferably living."

My mother paled. Piranhas had never been part of her experience, so she asked me, "Well, don't they have vegetarian ones?"

Now I paled. Oh no, no, said the look in my eyes as I threw protective arms in front of the aquarium. Those are the wimps. What I've got here is the real thing, the most dangerous species.

Since Joe wasn't actively dangerous at the moment, my parents quietly acquiesced, and I was able to turn my attention to the increasingly pressing business of feeding him.

There was a drainage ditch near my home that boasted a population of tiny minnows. I planned to catch them for Joe in the most sporting way I knew—using a bent pin and thread, with a piece of bread for bait. In quick time I hooked a good half dozen, then took them home in a pickle jar. As soon as I threw a minnow into the tank Joe's normally deadpan expression became bright with interest, as if he were saying, "What have we here?" I watched as he raised his eyes and fanned his pectoral fins, slowly rising from behind his rock. Then he headed for the minnow.

Joe's hunt was poetry in motion. The chase was neither chaotic nor haphazard. Joe didn't strike until he was sure of his target. I watched, my own mouth agape, as Joe circled his jaws about the minnow and—snap!—had his meal. Then Joe returned to his spot behind the rock to digest.

The commercial possibilities of Joe's feeding behavior didn't escape me. One day my mother came home to a line of neighborhood kids trailing out the front door and onto the sidewalk, each with twenty-five cents to buy a minnow from me to feed the piranha. The boys labeled the event "cool" and cheered Joe on. The girls thought it was disgusting (but they paid nevertheless). My mother, for her part, locked herself in the bathroom and turned on the faucets.

Joe grew and grew until he was considerably bigger than his rock. But his attachment to the rock never flagged. It was home base, the point of departure for every hunt. One of these feeding forays almost had horrendous consequences. It involved my little brother.

By the time Matthew was two, he had become just tall enough to reach the top of Joe's tank. One day I came home to find my sibling on tiptoes, dangling his fingers in the water. My eyes shot to the rock, but Joe wasn't there! And then I caught a flash of red and blue en route to Matthew's wriggling digits. I jumped after my brother, tackling him to the floor as Joe broke the surface of the water and then, frustrated, circled back to his rock.

That near-disaster was a portent of things to come. When Matthew turned three my mother threw him a birthday party and invited six or seven of his little friends. I was at school at the time. When I came home Joe's tank was brimming with popcorn and pretzels. From top to bottom it was a ten-gallon slush of junk food. I wanted to skin every one of the munchkins and save my brother for last. But the urgency of the situation left no time for fantasies. In a flash I dropped my books, fetched the net, and ran to the tank, where I fished around in the mess for my piranha, my friend. When I finally exhumed him, he was all but lifeless, barely able to raise his gill flaps. Matthew and his cohorts watched solemnly as I transferred Joe to the kitchen sink where, through some everlasting mercy, he came to in the chlorinated but fresh and oxygenated tap water.

I saw the writing on the wall. There wasn't enough room in the house for both a piranha and my brother. But my parents wouldn't listen to my pleas and insisted that I get rid of Joe. We had had three good years together, they told me, and now it was time to say goodbye.

The truth of the matter was that Joe had gotten awfully big, and he required the equivalent in minnows of a Big Mac a week. So I placed an ad in the paper:

> For Sale: Piranha!
> The Most Dangerous Species
> -$15-

The next day I got a call from a pet shop owner in the next town. He told me red piranhas were now hard to get so he'd buy Joe on the spot. He came over with a net and a bucket. When Joe saw him coming he hunkered down behind his rock. I could read the look in his eyes: "No! Hey! What's he doin' with that net?"

Joe put up a tremendous fight. He even bit through the net, forcing the buyer to beg my mother for a steel noodle strainer. In the end Joe landed in the bucket, where his teeth meant nothing to its thick plastic walls. The pet shop owner took out his handkerchief and wiped his forehead. "Phew!" he said. "Now I see how one of these suckers could eat Teddy Roosevelt."

I could hardly contain my tears as Joe was hauled off in such an undignified manner. I didn't even count the wad of bills the buyer had pressed into my hand. When I did later that night there was only twelve dollars. But I didn't care.

For two years I neither saw nor heard anything of Joe. Then, one day, I was walking down a street in the next town over and came to the shop owned by the man who had bought him. I almost flipped! There, in the window, was Joe, confined to a little five-gallon tank, over which a large sign had been posted. KIDS! FEED THE PIRANHA! $1.00!

Oh, Joe, I mourned. You've gone from glory in the Amazon to being a performer in a sideshow. And at that very moment he looked up at me as if to say, "How could you? How could you do this to me?"

That was the very last time I saw him. I guess he was flushed down a toilet, as happens with most pet fishes once they have outgrown their usefulness. In which case there is reason for hope. If it is true that alligators can live in sewers, then so can a hardy piranha. I believe those sewers are, in the long run, continuous with the wider and nobler waters of the Amazon, and that Joe, if he kept his wits about himself, found his way safely home.

A TRUCK FULL OF DREAMS AND ICE CREAMS

I could hardly believe my ears. But the music was unmistakable: a calliope rendition of "Turkey in the Straw," repeated over and over again, carried on the warm, still summer air.

I was tending the front garden when I heard it. And then I saw it: the white truck, cruising slowly into my Maine neighborhood. I stopped the machine and ran for my son. "Quick!" I called to Alyosha. "You won't believe this!"

Alyosha was loathe to leave his soccer goal, where he had been practicing his kick for the past half hour, but he sensed this was important to me, and so he came along. We stood shoulder to shoulder by the side of the street. Alyosha had never seen a Good Humor truck before, but I was instantly filled with memories of the New Jersey summers of my childhood *defined* by its daily visit.

I signaled for the truck to stop. As we walked up to the service window a youngish, rather burly man leaned out. "What'll it be?"

I swallowed hard for both me and my son. "Are you from the past?" was all I managed.

The man laughed. "Why?" he asked.

He was too young to know, then. Too young to understand. I hadn't seen a Good Humor truck in perhaps fifteen years. Or maybe twenty. The idea of someone coming into your neighborhood to deliver ice cream was something we took for granted as kids living in urban New Jersey during the 1960s. Every summer evening, at or around 7:00 o'clock, Jack pulled around the corner and eased his white truck down the street, passing under a green canopy of sycamores and maples. By then we'd had a hard day of play and supper was over and done with. Ice cream seemed a fitting way—the only way—to cap things off.

Jack was a middle-aged man with slicked-back blond hair and quite a tummy. He wore an immaculate white uniform with a mechanical money changer clipped to his belt. As soon as he turned the corner and rang his rack of bells, we kids would quit our stickball game, disperse, make beelines for home, only to emerge a minute later with a dime or sometimes even a quarter clenched tightly in our sweaty little fists. Then we'd pile in front of Jack's service window while he admonished us not to push, not to shout, and to say "please" and "thank you."

He spoke fast and in a snapping manner, working his jaws in tandem with the tinny click of his money changer. He knew by heart every item in the truck's freezers and was up-to-the-moment on what was sold out and what was on special. Within ten minutes he had completed transactions with twenty to twenty-five kids and then, with an abrupt goodbye, was gone, jingling his way into the next neighborhood.

Needless to say, Jack commanded more attention and cooperation from us than our parents did. In fact, he had us on schedule. On those nights when I might be one of the few kids outside, Jack made no allowances. At the sound of his bells I had to break for the house, get the cash, and leap back onto the street in time for him to see me. On more than one occasion I chased after his truck, calling out "Jack! Wait up!", all the while squeezing the silver out of my dime.

As I think back on it, I realize how astute a businessman Jack was. You see, my cousin Kenny lived in a neighborhood eight blocks away but still part of Jack's territory. Sometimes, if I ordered a Toasted Almond or an ice cream sandwich for a dime, Jack would frown and jingle his money changer. "Your cousin Kenny spent a quarter," he'd cluck. And then, gullible as I was, I'd run home for fifteen more cents, while Jack called after me to hurry or else he'd leave.

When I was ten or eleven I remember wondering what Good Humor men did in the off-season. I had an image of all of them living together in the same house, sitting around in their white uniforms and white caps, wearing their money changers, comparing sales and arguing about which product was the best. Was it the Chocolate Eclair or the Creamsicle? Of course, I pictured Jack as the captain of the Good Humor men, keeping them organized, barking out orders, and telling them how much time to spend on each street.

Sadly, my neighborhood eventually fell victim to urban decay. In time, Jack disappeared as well. There was no announcement, no warning. He just stopped coming. As long as he was there, we still had a neighborhood. But shortly after losing him, families began to move out as well, as if, without Good Humor, there was no glue to hold the place together.

Alyosha still doesn't understand why I'm so excited about the appearance of the Good Humor man, but he's mesmerized by the pictures of the selections on the side of the truck. It takes at least a buck to do the trick now. Not so bad when you consider all that the Good Humor man brings to a place: music, conversation, and sweet licks. I ask the driver when he will be back. "Soon," he says. He tells me he's committed to making a go of it. I salute him and wish him well, resting my hand on the edge of his service window, reluctant to let him leave.

As the Good Humor man pulls away, I watch for a moment and am suddenly struck by the strongest impulse. Alyosha throws me a curious glance as I back away from him. Then I turn and scramble after the truck, running as I did when I was ten, coins jingling in my pocket, wanting to buy a Creamsicle, and a Chocolate Eclair, and a Humorette; wanting to stock up—just in case this really was a dream.

With the end of the school year approaching, I find myself in league with other parents—making arrangements for almost back-to-back summer activities for my young son, lest he find himself with a moment's free time on his hands with "nothing" to do.

Sometimes, as I pore over the brochures for swimming lessons, soccer camps, and summer music schools, I ask myself how this came to pass. What I mean is, how, in a single generation, did America make the leap from a culture in which summer meant true freedom for a child fresh out of school, to one in which the summer had to be as structured as a classroom?

Whatever happened to street games? In my New Jersey childhood of the sixties, summers seemed endless and anything but rushed because we kids were as busy as we wanted to be. We controlled our time because we were given the freedom to.

The games we played in the streets of my neighborhood were legion, handed down to us by our parents: stickball, dodgeball, hopscotch, bottle-caps, hide-and-seek, red rover. . . . But preeminent among these games was one called "stoop ball" or "points."

What a game! All that was required was a rubber ball and a set of front steps. The beauty of the game was that it could be played with as few as two people, especially valuable during those times when playmates were scarce.

The idea was this: the person with the ball stood in front of the steps while the other kids—the fielders—strung themselves out from sidewalk to street and onto the opposite sidewalk. The "batter" would then wind up and slam the ball against the stoop. If a fielder caught it, you were out, but if he missed, its distance determined whether you got a single, double, or triple. I was a solid double man myself, but Sal Briguglio had a great arm, and he'd get that ball to sail high and fast over the street and into the front yard of the house on the other side for a homer.

The important thing about stoop ball was that you had to find the right steps. My house had gray-painted cement ones with rounded edges. That was passable. But Mrs. Strenger next door had brick steps with hard, sharp edges. If you hit a riser, you could count on a base hit; but if you hit the edge, the ball rebounded with lightning speed, and you had a shot at a home run.

During those long, hot, brilliant summer days, we'd be out on the street by eight or eight-thirty in the morning and within fifteen minutes had some game or other going. By eleven there would be so many kids in the street and on the sidewalks that it's still amazing to me that we could decide upon anything at all. But we did. Between games we'd sometimes head for Mr. Riley's corner store, where the sweaty lot of us lined up along his counter for seven-cent cherry sodas served up in shapely little Coke glasses. After chortling the last of our sodas through paper straws, we'd stampede into the street again and set up for dodge-ball.

Other than those soda fountain breathers, the only breaks we'd take were a brief soup-and-sandwich lunch, and a supper preceded by the ululations of our parents from the windows of our homes, where they would shout for us (in four languages!) to come and eat while the food was still hot. After supper we'd be out on the street again for an evening stickball game thanks to the donation of some dad's broom handle. I remember my father once wrapping the end of one with electrical tape while we looked on in wonder at the precision work. "The grip is everything," my father told us as he handed over the stick. "Everything."

Nightfall meant little to us, except as a signal to break out the necessary tools for flashlight tag. Our parents relaxed in lawn chairs on the front porches of the all-but-conjoined homes, cautioning us every so often that it was getting late. Almost time to come in. "Just five more minutes!" we'd plead, and they'd nod. After an hour or two of this they'd finally draw the line and haul us into the house. We'd wash up, hit the sack, and in the morning awaken once again, every child competing to be the first on the street to get some game or other going.

What has happened to all of this? Why has the broom handle been replaced by the basketball camp that costs $385 a week?

I think there are two reasons. One is that the midsixties of which I speak was the absolute acme of the baby boom. There were kids everywhere, and families with four, five, six, or more children were not uncommon. This guaranteed ample playmates.

Second, life back then was still more of an external affair. The lack of air-conditioning in most homes meant that families got relief from the summer heat on the front porch. Further, television offered only a few channels, and there was little on for kids during the day. Neither were there computers or video games riveting kids to the living room floor. In short, the inside of the house was where a kid ate and slept and took baths; the street was where you had fun.

There are still kids around, of course, but now, with the privatization of summer activities, it costs money to play with them. It is a sad loss.

I live in Maine now. The other day, when my twelve-year-old son came home from school, he caught me knocking a rubber ball against our modest New England stoop. "What're you doin'?" he asked.

"Stoop ball," I told him. "Wanna play?"

"Nah," he frowned. "It looks boring."

Hauling back, I took steady aim and slammed one out and over the street. A homer!

"Tell it to Sal Briguglio!" I shouted after my son as he tooled away on his bike.

Boring? Not by a long shot.

WE SAVORED SUNDAY'S LEISURE

Impelled, perhaps, by a fit of spring ardor, I recently acted on impulse in a way that brought my thirteen-year-old son to roll his eyes.

It was a Sunday, bright and mild, on the waning edge of yet another long Maine winter. "Let's go for a drive," I announced as I hustled Alyosha toward the truck. "A Sunday drive."

"But *why*?" he whined. "Where are we going?"

After starting the truck I leaned toward the windshield and gestured. "Out there," I said. "Just out there." And we were off.

As a child growing up in New Jersey, Sunday was something to yearn for. I lived in a crowded, busy city, where the sights and sounds of commerce and industry were dizzying. Six days a week, that is. And then, on the seventh, Sunday dawned in silence, affording my town the tranquility of a sleepy village.

In short, Sunday once had a "feel" that set it apart from the other days of the week. It was a day of quiet, bacon and eggs on the stove, family visits, and church bells pealing in the distance. The high point of my childhood Sundays was the afternoon drive. My father owned a 1957 Chevy Bel Air (yellow and lime green) that gave him no end of trouble. But on Saturday evening he would suds up a bucket and lovingly wash the old girl down until she shone like a brand new haircut.

Come Sunday, my mother dressed me and my younger brother in shorts (weather permitting), freshly pressed shirts, and bow ties before planting us in the back seat of the Bel Air. Then she and my father took their places up front, and my dad maneuvered the boatlike vehicle down the narrow driveway and out onto the city street, navigating us toward the Palisades Parkway, high above the Hudson River.

I nose my own vehicle north, along Maine's Route 2, which in my neighborhood winds along one of the most beautiful rivers in the east, the Penobscot. "Ducks!" Alyosha announces. It's true, there are golden-eyes and mallards everywhere. I pull over for a few minutes so we can observe the birds as they glide upon the water. I explain to Alyosha the differences in coloration between the females and males. Then we ease back onto the road and continue north.

I recall one of the sublime thrills of driving along the Palisades with my family. Here and there, at lookouts over the Hudson, there were binocular telescopes mounted on steel posts (they're still there, last I checked). At the drop of a coin a child could wrap his arms around a machine and observe the far shore, the river below, and sailboats tacking north.

On the return journey, always at a leisurely forty-five miles per hour, my brother and I could sense the excitement building as we passed familiar landmarks. To the left, on the far side of the river—the Empire State Building. To the right, the railroad yards. And then, dead ahead, standing out against an otherwise drab and featureless turnpike, the bright orange and blue of a Howard Johnson's restaurant, our last stop before home. HoJo's meant a cheese dog and fries and an ice cream cone to savor on the return trip.

A little ways up the road from where Alyosha and I observed the ducks, there is a small ice cream stand, little more than a neatly painted shack. The owner is preparing to open for the season. I pull over, roll down my window and greet him. "Open yet?" I ask. He clucks his tongue, ready to answer in the negative. Then he sees my son's earnest face. "Oh," he says, "I'm sure I can scrape up something." Five minutes later we have two cones happily in hand (pistachio and maple walnut). We drive away, completely satisfied.

Alyosha and I rumble along in the truck, the windows cracked open to admit air freshened by last night's rain. To our left, the Penobscot surges; to our right, freshets pierce the pine woods. Pockets of ice and snow persist on the lee side of the trees. I slow to a stop and allow the engine to quietly idle as we seize this moment to observe the evidence of transition from one season to the next.

I am not yet convinced that Alyosha is happy to be on this Sunday drive, this journey without aim or object. But I take advantage of the quiet moment to ply him with questions about school, soccer, and his summer wish list. He eases back in his seat and considers each topic in turn. Then he makes his own contributions to the conversation.

We cross a bridge spanning the Penobscot, then coast down its western shore, so as to vary the route a bit. The trees on the eastern bank are illuminated by the lowering sun, the road before us is empty, and we arrive home with just enough Sunday left in our pockets to shoot some hoops in the backyard before the stars punctuate the end of a perfectly well-spent day, free for the taking.

The Sundays of my childhood were golden days. There was no urgency about them, and they unfailingly followed on the heels of every Saturday. As they were then, so can they be now, but I find that the week no longer drops them into my lap. It is up to me to seize them from the grasp of a busier world, as gifts to myself and to my son.

A Carbonated Blast from the Past

One recent, uncomfortably warm day, I was sitting on the back porch with my thirteen-year-old son. We knew there were things we could do to cool off, but the heat had imbued us with a stifling inertia. "I'd like to go swimming," Alyosha said, "but it's too hot to even get up."

I considered what my heart's desire of the moment would be. And then it came to me. "An ice cream soda," I voiced.

Alyosha threw me a quizzical look.

I returned his gaze. "A nice, cold, old-fashioned ice cream soda. That's what I'd like to have right now."

Alyosha tried to connect. "You mean a float?" he offered.

"Nope. An ice cream soda." I went on to tell him about Mr. Riley's corner store in my New Jersey town back in the sixties. How I'd go in there on hot summer days, and then watch, with eyes wide and mouth open, as Mr. Riley, with practiced skill, prepared an ice cream soda in a tall, fluted glass, jetting it up with seltzer until he had created a veritable Everest of foam half again as big as the glass itself. "I don't think I've had a real ice cream soda since then," I concluded.

"Why not?" my son asked. "Don't they make them anymore?"

I nodded reflectively. "Oh, they make them," I said, "but not like they used to."

Alyosha rolled his eyes. I could read his expression: Oh no, not another "not like they used to" story from Dad. But before he could escape I had whisked him off in my truck. "Where are we going?" he begged.

"You'll see."

Within a few minutes we pulled up in front of Pat's, a small restaurant in my central Maine town. Pat's has been there since 1931, and very little about the place has changed. If anyone could make an ice cream soda in the strict sense of the phenomenon, they could.

When we walked in, Alyosha headed straight for a booth, but I preempted him. "Oh, no," I corrected, "over here." I led him to the counter and directed him to take a stool. "You've got to sit at the counter for an ice cream soda," I lectured. "And you've got to rest your elbows on the countertop, like this." Alyosha watched skeptically as I demonstrated the technique. Then I gave the place the once-over: ceiling fans, linoleum tile floor (well worn), wooden booths, tin ceiling, soda fountain. The ambience was perfect.

A waitress approached on the opposite side of the counter. "What'll you boys have?" she asked as she arranged our place settings.

"May I ask you a question?" I ventured.

She nodded.

"How long have you worked here?"

Sandy—I later learned her name—cracked a beguiling smile.

"You wouldn't believe me if I told you."

"Try me."

"Since 1961."

"Perfect!" I exclaimed, turning the heads of several patrons. "Listen," I continued, leaning across the counter. "Can you make an ice cream soda?"

Sandy waved me off. "Are you kidding? Of course."

I rolled my hands in anticipation and began to enumerate the ingredients: "Vanilla ice cream, chocolate syrup, a dash of cream . . ."

"And seltzer," said Sandy, picking up the beat.

"In a fluted glass?"

"The tall ones?"

"Yes. And how about paper straws?"

Sandy frowned. "We use plastic now. Can't get the paper straws any-more."

Well, one couldn't have everything. "Ma'am," I announced, sitting bolt upright on my stool, "two ice cream sodas."

Alyosha had watched the negotiations with all the focus of a specta-tor at Wimbledon. Now both he and I looked on as Sandy prepared our treats with a panache that would have done Mr. Riley proud. First the ice cream, then the syrup, cream, and finally, before our very eyes, she placed the glasses under the fountain head, yanked on the handle, and discharged a violent stream of seltzer, creating a froth that took me back thirty years in the instant.

Sandy placed the sodas before us, stepped back, and folded her hands. She hovered, watching anxiously, as I directed Alyosha to take a sip. "What do you think?" I asked after his first taste of the ambrosia.

Alyosha swallowed, turned his eyes to me, and nodded. "Good," he pronounced.

I quickly seized my straw and, with one eye on Sandy, took my own inaugural sip.

A few seconds passed. "Dad," prompted Alyosha, breaking the silence. And then, "Dad?"

Still bent over my soda, I slowly turned my face to him.

"How is it?" he asked.

I nodded, first to my son, and then to Sandy. "Alyosha," I said, barely able to speak, "I am so happy now that I could burst."

And that's how Sandy came to tell the story of the five- dollar tip for a check that came to only two dollars and fifty cents.

I GOT THE MOON AND THE STARS THAT YEAR

I don't think I've ever seen more beautiful night skies than those that overlie the state of Maine. Until I came north some eighteen years ago, I didn't quite know what people meant when they described stars so nu-merous and bright as to illuminate the landscape below. Now that I have experienced it for myself, I seize every opportunity to observe the firmament.

Just this morning, before daybreak, awaking from a restless sleep, I opened my eyes to the morning star—a Venus so brilliant that I thought I must be dreaming. But a few squints later it still sparkled through the cold December air. I stared in wonder until morning's first light erupted on the horizon, washing the planet away.

Sometimes, when I consider my affinity for the night sky, I feel as if I am making up for lost time. I grew up in urban, industrialized New Jersey, under a scrim of city lights and a veil of factory effluvia. Only the most determined stars and planets managed to wink through: the moon, of course; Venus, Jupiter, and Saturn at their brightest; the Big Dipper and Orion. Beyond this there was only the occasional star, perhaps the brightest member of a team constituting some other constellation, divorced from the pattern that gave it meaning.

This didn't stop me from asking my parents for a telescope for my tenth Christmas. I had recently made the transition from career chemist to aspiring astronomer, so my request was a logical one. My parents, ever-willing to stoke the fires of my curiosity, dutifully presented me with a reflecting telescope on Christmas morning—a three-inch mirror in a black cardboard tube, with folding metal tripod. I was, in a word, thrilled.

The frustrating thing about receiving a telescope at the crack of dawn is that one has to wait until nightfall to put it to good use. In the interim, I took it into the front room and aimed it across the street through the living room window of the Rutiglianos and observed them as they celebrated their own Christmas with their three boys—Charlie, Vito, and Vinnie. "Wow," I announced to my family while squinting through the scope, "Vito got a Robot Commando!" I could also count the raviolis that Mrs. Rutigliano was making by hand in the kitchen. Such was the power and resolution of my new celestial tool.

I waited with bated breath all through that Christmas Day. There was a crust of snow on the ground, and the windowpanes were bordered with frost. As evening approached it became even colder, but this didn't daunt me in the least. By five o'clock it was dark enough to run outside with my telescope. I hit the street, looked up, and bit my lip when I saw that the streetlights were preempting most of the first stars. But there was a three-quarter moon on the rise, and my heart took flight.

I hightailed it to the end of the street, a dark corner where a lamp had burned out some days before. I set up my tripod on an icy snowbank and aimed it at the moon, laying the side of my face against the outside of the tube to deadsight the satellite. Then I brought my eager eye to the viewing lens and was immediately rewarded with a flood of lunar light. I carefully turned the plastic focusing knob until, in crisp relief, I captured the moon, as crumpled as a sheet of used tinfoil. I was open-mouthed at the sight of my first crater—Tycho—a brilliant, flowerlike splat on the moon's northern aspect. I remained outside that night, observing the moon over and over again, until my fingers and toes ached with the cold. Then I returned home, utterly in love.

By the next day I had regained my scientific poise and objectivity to the point where I had made a bold and enterprising sign to hang on my scope: SEE THE MOON AND STARS FOR A NICKEL! That night was even colder than the previous one, but cold skies tend to be clear skies, and I found myself standing on my street corner, open for business, with a modest basket of stars overhead.

While waiting for my first customers, I pressed my eye to the cold lens of my telescope and commenced a grand tour of everything worth seeing. I first passed over the surface of the now-familiar moon. Having established my bearings, I headed for more remote regions, beginning with the Big Dipper, coursing along its handle and using it as a springboard to bound off for Orion. There I scanned first-magnitude stars with marvelous names like Rigel and Betelgeuse, the latter a red giant. Traversing the vast interstellar distances with unfathomable speed, I arrived at Taurus, where I orbited the Pleides, a loose cluster of stars and gas known as the "Seven Sisters." Then came Aldebaran, Polaris, Sirius, and, as I recall, Vega.

I remained outside for the longest time, to the point where I had forgotten what I had come for. By the time my father laid a hand on my shoulder to coax me in, I was ready to pack up my observatory. And so I tucked the telescope under my arm and ambled home with my dad. I hadn't earned a nickel, but as my travels that night had taught me, the universe is a hard thing to pin a price on.

My father is a firm believer that a good hardware store is good for the spirit. I couldn't agree more. There is something about the commingling of wood, metal, adhesives, and assorted doodads which affirms that, in a world which can sometimes seem doubtful and tentative, there still exist solutions to many of our daily problems.

In my small Maine town we have a hardware store that has been in business since 1892. Its lived-in ambience lies in the squeak of the oak floor when one enters from the street; in the aging black lab whose welcoming lick discriminates against no hand; in the sagging tin ceilings; and in the cross-breeze that passes over the seed bins in March, offering a preliminary whiff of spring while snow still lies about.

Park's Hardware, by some grace, has persisted in its main street storefront despite the arrival of the monolithic home repair warehouses. Some call it a miracle, but to me the reason is clear, manifested not only in the fact that it is a place where one can still buy a single screw for two cents (instead of being blackmailed into picking up a box of a hundred), but in a scene I witnessed there about a year ago.

A young college student had just moved into her apartment. She approached one of the employees and confided that she couldn't open her one and only closet. "It takes a skeleton key," she lamented. "Where on earth am I going to get a skeleton key?"

Without hesitation, the employee stepped past the young woman and opened a flat drawer in an old wooden cabinet. He reached in and grabbed a handful of skeleton keys. "There were only a few different types," he explained as he placed them in her hand. "Take these and try them. When you find the one that fits, just bring the others back."

The student reached for her purse, but the employee waved her off. "No," he said. "Pay me when you find the key that fits."

"You're kidding," she said, not realizing that trust was part of the transaction. As she left, a hint of disbelief still lingered on her face.

Such small dramas have little chance of occurring in the warehouses, where it is every man for himself and the job of the hired help is simply to exchange cash for goods in as expeditious a way as possible. In Park's, by contrast, a purchase often takes the form of a consultation, where a problem is presented ("How do I drill a hole in a brick?") and the employee and customer arrive at a mutually satisfactory solution.

The thing is, small, locally owned hardware stores *know* things. One need only state one's predicament to set the wheels of creativity in motion. I once walked into Park's with two pieces of plumbing, the opposite ends of a system that stretched for ten feet under the house. "How do I get from here," I asked, holding out one piece of metal, "to here?", as I presented the other.

Lin, the owner, looked the parts over. "Hmmm," he pondered, hand to chin, and then his eyes caught fire. We hightailed it to the plumbing section and for the next twenty minutes rummaged through plastic bins of pipe, faucets, junctions, and valves. "This is fun!" I finally blurted out, like a ten-year-old, as a clearly unconventional contraption slowly took shape before my eyes. "And it'll work," said Lin by way of confirmation. "That's even funner."

Despite the cramped space (a hardware store worth its salt *must* be cramped), Lin has judiciously made room for two old chairs where customers can sit while waiting their turn, or simply bide their time and observe the passing parade.

One warm summer day I availed myself of this opportunity to sit and watch and listen as people came and went, their needs as personal and unique as they were: a professional carpenter who knew exactly what he wanted; a student looking for a screw for his license plate; an elderly woman wondering how to remove gum from a carpet; and a lady whose request sounded like a Haiku ("Marigold seeds / a large pack / variegated / keep the cats away").

When my father visits from New Jersey he looks for any justification to go to Park's. A restless do-it-yourselfer by nature, he believes that a good hardware store, in addition to being good for the spirit, is the inveterate tinkerer's natural habitat. On his last visit, he clucked his tongue at my leaky bathroom faucets. Then he headed to Park's, returning a good while later with a washer, which he dutifully installed. "But the other faucet's still leaking," I pointed out. "Why didn't you get two washers?"

Smiling, and with anxious anticipation, he said, "Oh, I thought I had. I guess I'll have to go back to the hardware store."

Long may it reign.

I make no secret of the absolute despair I feel when I see whole stores devoted to the sale of something that once occupied a modest corner of main street clothing stores.

When did such a simple affair as shopping for sneakers become something akin to mounting a scientific expedition? Where once there existed only low-tops and high-tops, there are now medium-tops, booties, and sneakers with personal liners; running, walking, and bicycling sneakers; and basketball, tennis, squash, and racketball sneakers; and even sneakers that wink at you with a maddening incandescence whenever the foot is put down.

I was recently drawn into one of these footware emporia by my teenage son, Alyosha, who has a well-honed taste for the things. "Thirty dollars," I kept reciting, like a mantra, declaring the limit of what I would spend for something designed to wear out within a month.

How naive of me. The lowest price on any of the sneakers was a cool $55. And that was a sale item marked down from $89.99. My son casually slipped the shoe from its little acrylic shelf, and within a twinkling, as if he had tripped a silent alarm, a young woman was at our side. "Are you interested in that one?" she asked.

Alyosha made puppy-dog eyes at me, and the woman immediately picked up the beat. "I'll have a tech come right over," she said before moving away.

A tech? Sure enough, a young athletic-looking man of college age approached us. He laid his hand on the shoe and began to recite its attributes, describing its chemical composition, its unique means of supporting the ankle, and the particular freedom it rendered the toes. "And the middle layer," he said, fairly quivering with excitement, "is the latest composite polymer designed to resist cracking and to increase the integrity of the lining." Then he looked up at me as the bearer of the credit card. "So what do you think?"

I was glad he asked. I threw up my hands. "It's a *foot*, for goodness' sake," I lamented. "All we want to do is cover a foot."

The salesman looked like an ancient who had just been told that the earth revolves around the sun. Even Alyosha glared at me as if to say, "How could you embarrass me like this?"

Well, it comes naturally, as a result of my own formative experience. When I was a kid growing up in Jersey City, sneakers were sold in the back of the local clothing store downtown. There were two types: the

$2.98 ones—low black canvas with a plastic toe—and the crown jewel of sneakers, the hallowed Converse, selling for $9.98 (and no sales tax).

Family finances being what they were, the Converse remained out of reach for me for the longest time, and I contented myself with the cheaper footware which, if well cared for (and so long as the foot didn't grow), would easily last from one summer to the next.

But I could still admire the Converse and regard it with hungry eyes. It was the white Chuck Taylor All-Star high-tops that bespoke quality and promised spectacular changes in the young athlete. Only one boy on my block wore them—Sal Briguglio—but he was the best stickball player I'd ever known. What more evidence did one need?

I was sixteen when I got my first pair of Converse, and that more than anything else told me that I had arrived. I remember putting them on in the store, walking around to test the fit, and feeling, at long last, like a pro.

Under Yuletide duress, I bought Alyosha his $55 sneakers with the zipper instead of laces and the fabric covering instead of vinyl or that wonderful Converse canvas. By the end of the first week of basketball practice, the linings of both shoes were torn up. We brought them back to the store. When the sneaker tech approached us I reported that the magic middle layer of polymers hadn't done its job. We then exchanged them for a more traditional—and durable—shoe.

That evening, while noodling around on the Web, I stumbled upon the site for the Converse company. I was almost beside myself, having thought that the hallowed sneaker had gone the way of the dodo. When I clicked on the listing for the Chuck Taylor All-Star model, I was immediately rewarded with an image of the shoe I had loved, with its ankle patch bearing the Converse blue star, and the blue and white lines running around that thick rubber sole.

I called Alyosha over to the screen. "This," I said, throwing my arm out in presentation, "is the greatest sneaker ever made."

My son drew his face close to the screen and then shook his head. "Did you wear these?" he asked.

"Proudly."

"It figures."

I watched as Alyosha slipped away in his new sneakers, the ones with all the glitter and no promise. And then I turned back to the image of my Chuck Taylor Converse All-Stars. I touched the screen and ran my finger along its classic contours. And man oh man, I swear I could feel the give of the rubber and the scratch of the canvas. And if I inhaled deeply and held it in, I could smell that new sneaker smell, that fresh-out-of-the-box smell, the aroma of that classic sneaker that carried Sal Briguglio—and then me—through many a stickball summer, as if we had wings.

DRAWN TO A DOWNPOUR'S EXUBERANCE

The other day, with little warning, there was a cloudburst. My thirteen-year-old son and I were in the house at the time, and I, at least, was content to watch the show from warm and dry quarters. But suddenly, before I knew what was happening, Alyosha burst through the door and ran out into the backyard, his arms extended, his face turned heavenward as he spun happily about in the heavy, driving curtains of rain.

And then I did the thing which still puzzles me. I ran to the door and yelled for him to come inside. "You'll get wet!" I called out, ridiculously. "Get in here right now."

Alyosha only smiled, as it was clear that he was already soaked to the skin and wasn't going to get any wetter.

What was it that compelled me to react with alarm to a boy relishing a downpour? Now that I think of it, this could be one of those markers that separates child from adult: in times of sudden rain, adults scurry for shelter, while children jump for joy and catch the raindrops on their tongues.

I remember, as a boy in New Jersey, monumental cloudbursts, accompanied by thunderclaps that shook the windowpanes, and expansive bolts of lightning that scribbled their way across dark, boiling skies.

During those summer storms, we kids walked the streets until the cuffs of our sopping jeans were dragging under our heels. Sometimes we'd get off a game of stickball for the added excitement of whacking the ball in tandem, or sometimes coincident with, a rumble of thunder from above. During all of this, our parents were separated from us by porches or storm windows, gazing out at their progeny—their water babies—and placidly accepting the counsel of the years, having no more inclination to run out into the rain than to swing from a tree limb.

The more intense and spontaneous a summer storm is, the shorter its duration tends to be. But sometimes this theory is put to the test, as it was one day when I was about twelve. Rain had been predicted, but not the protracted, relentless downpour that actually took place. Eventually the streets became rivers, with the currents coursing purposefully along the curbs, taking all manner of objects with them: sticks, newspapers, balls, a windblown hat . . . all of it carried to wherever it is that rain freshets go.

And, of course, we kids went wading into the ankle-high water as well. For a city kid, it was like having a river come to your doorstep, a gift of cool respite from a hot, sticky summer day. Eventually the water got as high as our calves, and one of my cousins and I, already soaked clean through, were inspired to inflate our bright yellow, navy surplus, two-man raft, in which we set out through our urban neighborhood, paddling door to door. As we passed romping groups of other children, they waved to us and begged for rides.

As for the adults, they stood or sat out on their island porches and stoops, high and dry, shaking their heads at us, feigning disdain, although who's to say that somewhere deep inside they didn't long to join us?

And then, sometime during my high school career, all of this stopped, and I, too, became one of the "drys"—a rain-runner who seeks shelter when the first chill drop strikes the bare, sensitive skin of the back of my neck.

These memories came back to me while watching my son do his rain dance out on the back lawn. I watched as his sopping clothes hung about his lean, washboard body like wet laundry thrown over a fence. I settled back onto my heels, composed once again, harboring a bit of regret for something—whatever it is—that I had lost in the transition from boy to man.

Suddenly, Alyosha called out to me. "You're chicken, Dad!" he taunted through a bright smile. "You're too chicken to come out!"

That did it. Girding myself, I discarded shoes and socks and tore out through the door, catching my son after only a minute's chase. I held him tight as both of us laughed in the rain.

Perhaps, as has been said, you can't go home again. But it's sometimes nice to visit.

The other night I participated in something I thought had all but disappeared from our midst: a group of fathers playing—riotously—with their young sons.

Such sights have become a rarity. In an age where life seems to be leading us rather than vice versa, I had almost forgotten what it was like to be in the company of men and boys and to pretend, for a little while, that we didn't have a care in the world besides each other.

What happened was this. My thirteen-year-old son Alyosha was playing in an indoor soccer league. Normally, the boys were cheered on by dads and/or moms during these low-key, off-season games. But on this particular evening only the dads were in the stands. What's more, the game was a late one. We fathers watched our sons garner a sweet victory over a tough opposing team, and then, although it was already nine-thirty, a striking thing happened: the kids remained on the field and signaled to us to come down and play, fathers against sons.

We looked at one another for a long moment, until the spark of "Why not?" flashed in our eyes. Before you knew it we had cocked our ballcaps around, and an out-of-shape gaggle of middle-aged professional spectators stampeded down the bleachers and onto the field, where we took up our uncertain positions opposite our sons. A whistle blew, the ball was kicked, and the game was joined.

The thing is, I *remember* this stuff from my own boyhood. I *remember* my father coming home after already having spent a full day at work, then stripping off his coat and tie to throw a ball to eight or nine of us kids. Then other fathers would join, as a way of unwinding, of showing that they had missed us that day, of making a contribution to the neighborhood.

As the soccer game took off, it was clear that our sons had the edge in speed and practiced teamwork, but we dads were far craftier. We swept the field with the ball, grunting and puffing with our exertions, crying out, "I'm open!" "Man on!" "Cross! Cross!"

Suddenly, I had the ball. I stumbled along with it as the boys set up their defenses. "Man on!" cried one of the dads, and I looked behind me to see my own son closing in like a bird of prey. No match for his speed, I kicked the ball and sent the game off in another direction.

When I was a kid we didn't have indoor soccer and Astroturf. We had stickball and asphalt. On warm summer evenings, just as a game was experiencing a lull, our dads would come out, clapping their hands to liven up the game. We laughed as we watched them spruce up old skills with alacrity, as if our game were the one they had been waiting for all their lives. I recall my father standing over home plate (a manhole cover) with bat (a broom handle) in hand. We taunted him good-naturedly, then watched slack-jawed as he sent the ball sailing over the tops of the sycamores.

I don't recall ever getting tired back then. During this soccer game, though, we old-timers were nearly exhausted after only ten minutes of play; but our boys would have ridiculed us mercilessly if we had abandoned our drive, so we persisted until we had somehow maneuvered the ball close to their goal. Then we did the unorthodox—we brought our whole team forward, including the goalie, and hammered their goal relentlessly until we scored. We scored!

Unfortunately, our goal served to make the boys doubly determined. In quick time they planted one in our goal. It was now tied up.

We elders were on our last legs. One dad bent down to tie his shoe. Another looked for a place to stow his ballcap, while a third took a few moments to inspect the condition of the Astroturf. All of these stall tactics bought us a second wind, and soon we were off again, plodding freighters driving up against the imperial navy of youth.

Once again we moved as a real team (of sorts); once again we cheered one another on and laughed even as our sons laughed at us; and once again we barked out the requisite, breathless directives: "Pass!" "Dribble!" "Chip it!" "Cross! Cross!"

Someone did cross, and once again the ball came to me. I dribbled, tripped, stumbled, recovered—and I scored!

Then the boys scored.

And then they scored again, for the win.

A cheer went up, and fathers and sons ran to one another, with backslaps and hugs all around.

It was right and just that our sons won that game, for they are the ones who move with the speed and agility we fathers once possessed and have now—gracefully, I like to think—surrendered. It was the poet Jon Swan who wrote:

> To have lived long enough to have flown
> and to have given up flight.
> To take one's turn in the circle of fathers.

On that evening of our sweet soccer loss, I finally understood what it must have been like for my dad to be part of that noble band.

OUR STOOP WAS STUPENDOUS

The other day I overheard a student in the university where I teach shouting down the hallway to someone: "I'll leave the envelope out on my stoop!"

I immediately went up to her and asked what part of New York or New Jersey she was from. She looked surprised. "How did you know?" she asked, and then identified Brooklyn as her childhood home.

It was the word *stoop* that gave her away. I've been living in Maine for eighteen years now, and it has occurred to me that people up here don't say "stoop." They say "steps" or "porch." I immediately made the rounds of transplanted friends from Texas, Minnesota, California and Georgia, confronting them with the query, "What's a stoop?"

All of them drew a blank. The Texan's innocent response: "A dull-witted person?"

That was it, then. The stoop, or stairs, leading to the front door of a home, seemed to be a term familiar only to people like me who grew up in the greater New York metropolitan area. It made me wonder how many times I had said "stoop," only to confuse the Mainers I was talking to.

Ah, the stoop. It wasn't just a set of concrete or brick steps fronting a house. It was a royal court where so much of the daily business of my urban New Jersey neighborhood was conducted. It was the throne upon which Mabel Churney sat in her faded housedress, day after summer day, sipping iced tea, perched for an opportunity to report wayward kids to their parents. It was the place where we played "stoop ball," bouncing a rubber ball off the steps to "fielders" in the street beyond. It was the quiet sanctum of my boyhood where, on early July mornings, I sat and read "Archie" comic books while languidly chewing a box of Mike 'n Ikes, waiting for my friends to emerge.

Where on earth did this word originate? Did it come from the steps which constitute the stoop? Or was it derived from the image of someone stooping down to pick up the morning paper? The dictionary states, simply and directly, that a stoop is "a porch, platform, entrance stairway, or small veranda at a house door."

This cannot, and never will, do the stoop justice. It does not take into account the central role of the stoop in the urban neighborhood, especially on hot summer evenings before air-conditioning was looked upon as a necessity. Congregating on the stoop was a social function which brought pleasures no dictionary's terse prose can appreciate.

Picture my neighborhood. Brick, shingled, and stucco houses standing shoulder to shoulder on both sides of the street. No two homes exactly alike. But all of them were fronted by a stoop which extended itself like a vast lap, bidding one to stay a while, sit for a chat, and observe and comment on the passing scene.

The stoop of my boyhood home was flanked by concrete balustrades, each of which was crowned with a large cement urn containing my mother's autumn joy sedum with its rust red blossoms. Such decoration lent dignity and a bit of flair to the modest home of a working-class family in those days. It also gave our stoop a kind of regal flourish, befitting those who felt inclined to hold forth on neighborhood politics, or those who just wanted a place to sit and rest. Once, when I was seven or so, I spotted a stranger, an old man, reposing there and ran back through the door to tell my mother. She took a peek, went into the kitchen, and, a moment later, handed me a tall glass of cool water to give to the man. He accepted it gratefully, drank, and went on his way.

I find myself wondering if they still build houses with stoops. I find it hard to believe. The trend, after all, has been for people to put more space between one another rather than gather in such blatantly public places. In this light, the deck has replaced the stoop, and rather than being in front of the house, it is hidden around the back, where no one but the inhabitants have routine access to it. This is a tragic loss and a lonely thing. I think that even the solitary but companionable Thoreau, if he were with us today, would prefer the stoop to the deck.

These thoughts have been on my mind for quite some time now. So much so that when I went out to get today's paper at first light, I detoured around to the front of my house to take a look at my own situation. There, flush up against the front door, was that single, modest brick slab with its two steps, a mere pallet designed only for lifting a person to the threshold. Nevertheless, I sat there, in the dim morning light and in the cold, and I closed my eyes, and I suddenly saw my family gathered there, and my relatives and friends, all laughing, telling stories, and sighing with pleasure at the relief afforded by a summer breeze.

"Dad!"

I gave a start. It was my fourteen-year-old son, fresh out of bed, calling from inside the house.

"Dad! Where are you?"

Pulling myself together and closing my collar against the cold, I shouted back, "I'm out on the stoop!"

You'll never know how good it felt to say that again.

TRAVELS

I have had the unique experience of visiting Iceland both at the height of summer, when sunset is of but a moment's duration, and in the depths of winter, when day consists of a tentative, three-hour sky-glow, following which the whole of the land is again doused in a darkness laced with the recurring howl of North Atlantic winds.

Iceland in winter is strictly an Icelandic game—so much so that at one party I attended in Reykjavík a large, dark man came swaggering toward me through the crowd of guests, threw his arm about my shoulder, and when I told him I wasn't an Icelander, asked incredulously, "Then what on earth are you doing in Iceland?"

I was en route to visit friends in a village on the edge of the Greenland Sea, where the black ocean lies frozen to a beach of black volcanic sand. But what was most interesting of all was the long bus trek north, a ride my friends in Reykjavík told me would take "six hours. Or twenty hours. It depends on the weather. But don't worry."

I didn't. I was in good company. Every available seat on the bus was taken, and some of the farewells in Reykjavík were as protracted and poignant as emigrant leave-takings from the Old World must have been.

We departed the capital in the darkness of early morning, and as we left the city limits a soft snow began to fall as Mozart's *Clarinet Concerto* seeped from overhead speakers. Children slept, conversations were muted and expressions reserved, in true Nordic fashion. I settled into my situation as if it were a warm bath.

The road north, being snow-laden, was indistinguishable from the bordering fields, with which it fused in a broad, white expanse of desolation. Our driver followed in the tracks of previous vehicles. I wondered what guide there was in those instances when time and snow had filled in such fortunate clues.

When the sky turned from black to royal blue with wisps of tangerine drawn out against it, the surrounding landscape became more apparent and breathtaking. Our eastern and western horizons were bounded by snow-covered mountains. Between them, in the valley of our transit, only more snow, slung from those mountains in a meld of unbroken whiteness. It was like riding the back of an endless cloud. Here and there a black line snaked its way through the snow—cut by the relative warmth of some underlying stream.

I began to think of the times I had flown over such far-flung, seemingly forlorn places as Labrador, Greenland, and Lapland. "Is there really life down there?" I would ask myself. And then, in the middle of some tree-less plain—a house. That meant human activity, perhaps a family. Ah, if only my eyes were telescopic: what must their lives be like?

The bus hissed as the brakes were applied, and we rolled to a long, slow stop. A few voices were raised. I looked out my window again and saw that the wind had picked up some snow from the surrounding fields and tossed it into the air like talcum.

The doors opened and a young mother and her little boy, perhaps three years old, got off. The bus hummed steadily in place for some mo-ments as I watched, as we all watched, the two of them walk down into a seemingly eternal field, hand in hand into the snow cloud, until they had disappeared. At that moment I heard the low drone of a plane di-rectly overhead. I looked up and nodded.

Even in the isolating dark and cold of the Icelandic north there is life. There is warmth.

Then the bus pressed ahead.

ICELAND REDUX, WITH SON

I recently realized a long-held dream of taking my son to a mystical place.

I first went to Iceland in 1983, in a fever of abandon from the tedium of graduate studies. I needed to get away for a while, and the far reaches of the earth seemed an appropriate destination.

Actually, there was more to it than that. Iceland had long ago captured my imagination. The very idea of a people thriving on a volcanic, sub-arctic rock, speaking the same language as the Vikings, and enduring half the year in darkness appealed to the adventurer in me. And so I went.

I arranged through the Icelandic Ministry of Agriculture to live for a summer on a farm in the far north of the country, in a river valley first settled a thousand years ago. For three months preceding my trip I cor-responded with the farmer who would be my host. Eggert's letters were in impeccable English, so it was easy for me to communicate my desire to learn as much Icelandic as possible during my stay. At that point I had been studying the language from tapes and had managed to commit only two phrases to memory: "It is not good to kill many men," and "Isn't the odor splendid!"

After flying to Keflavík, I boarded a bus for the six-hour ride north. I told the bus driver to let me off at "Sveinsstadir" or "Pig Place," as Eggert, my Icelandic farmer, had instructed me to.

The bus threaded its way northward along the west coast of Iceland. I was struck by a landscape devoid of trees or other softening features. Iceland was made of rock, and bare precipices and ledges were everywhere—an unforgiving landscape embellished as if by intent with dreamily placed cloud bands, waterfalls, and steam vents releasing wisps of vapor out of the earth.

Six hours after our departure the bus suddenly stopped. The driver announced "Sveinsstadir" and handed me my backpack as I disembarked. I watched forlornly as the bus rumbled away, still farther north. Then it was gone.

I looked around me and saw nothing but dark, volcanic mountains, the hard-packed dirt road we had traveled, a briskly flowing stream, and a haze of grass on a broad meadow in which a scattering of sheep grazed. There wasn't even a pig to validate the place name. From all appearances I was the last person on earth.

And then, seemingly out of nowhere, a Land Rover pulled up. The young woman driver nodded toward me. Without a word I got in, and in absolute silence we drove forty miles through the heart of a river valley as green as anything in Ireland. We arrived at a simple farmhouse and went in. An older woman—the mother—ushered me to the kitchen table and put some cake in front of me. The daughter sat as well. Then her three younger brothers joined the group. For the next thirty minutes we sat together, no one uttering a syllable. They simply stared at me as I nibbled at the cake. I was in Iceland and felt cut off in time and distance from everything I knew.

The silence was broken when Eggert burst through the door. Big-boned, broad-shouldered, and with a great gray mane of disheveled hair, he swung a passel of trout onto the table, which brought great commotion to the family. Then he threw his hand out to me and said, "Welcome to Iceland!"

I was more moved by the sound of English than by Eggert's sentiment. "I'm so happy you speak English," I said. But Eggert just shrugged. I quickly realized he couldn't speak English. Later I learned that a friend of his in Reykjavík had written all those perfect letters to me.

Before I had much of a chance to think of the home I had left behind I was fully immersed in the eternal work of the farm. It was the hardest and longest work I had ever done, but evenings spent strolling along the river or riding horseback under the midnight sun were ample reward for my labors. Within a very few days I had come to think of Eggert's family as mine, too. I was in Iceland, living as an Icelander, and even learning to speak Icelandic. I was at the ends of the earth, but I felt as if I were at the center of the world.

That was many years ago. Now I have a son. I promised myself that I would give him the gift of feeling comfortable in the world beyond his own backyard. Thirteen years after my inaugural visit I boarded a plane with Alyosha, age eleven, and we flew north over the Atlantic. The closer we drew to Iceland the more my anticipation rose.

We settled in with friends in Reykjavík, who told Alyosha of all the wonders and adventures that lay ahead of him. All the while he stared out their window at a soccer field filled with children. The next thing I knew, he was on that field, undaunted by new faces and an indecipherable language. For the next five days he played soccer until midnight, when I finally felt obligated to drag him away from his newfound friends, even though the sun was still burning above the horizon.

All of my energies and aspirations were focused on taking Alyosha north, to Eggert's farm, the place where I had first experienced the allure and power of Iceland. We made the same six-hour bus trip I had taken years ago, arriving at the farm in early evening. The children were grown and had moved away, but Eggert and his wife, Hjördis, greeted us with warmth and accepted Alyosha as a member of the family.

The landscape hadn't changed. The hills were still treeless but green with grass; the salmon river flowed briskly behind the farmhouse; sheep wandered over the meadows; and the most intense silence reigned. But while my emotional response to this homecoming was poignant, Alyosha was beside himself with boredom. I took him on a hike to a waterfall. We observed salmon from a precipice. We skipped rocks on the river. All to no avail. By the second day of our stay he was almost in tears.

And then it struck me: This was my place, not his. It was special to me because I had brought so much to it. When I offered my son an opportunity to catch the next bus to Reykjavík he was elated, and I too felt, for his sake, a palpable relief.

The next morning we headed south. Six hours later, Alyosha was on that Reykjavík soccer field again, hobnobbing with a gaggle of tow-headed Icelandic boys, laughing his heart out and scoring occasional goals. We did manage to squeeze in a geyser here and a volcano there, but when we returned home and my son's friends asked him about Iceland, his response was singular: he had played soccer under the midnight sun.

I have my Iceland, and Alyosha has his.

FIVE DAYS IN YUGOSLAVIA

The trip to Yugoslavia, when it was Yugoslavia, had been a whim. I had been next door in Italy at the time, and so, I thought, why not? I knew I had a distant relative there, an old woman living in one of those vowelless places that dot the country. The romance of traveling to an island called "Krk" took me by storm, and I surrendered blindly to the impulse.

I recall riding the boat through the canals of Venice, the train through the dark mountains of Slovenia and down to the warm Croatian Adriatic, the ferry to the island, and the long walk along a dirt road, past laughing schoolgirls, bright cottages, gardens brimming with roses, and a kerchiefed grandmother prodding her ox along with a stick, calling it "my sweet." When I paused, unsure of my way, an old bear of a man in a worn tweed coat noticed my disorientation, threw his arm around my shoulders, and said, "I will take care of you. Don't worry."

I didn't. How could I? The people I had thus far met were as agreeable as the landscape and the weather: warm, welcoming, their faces etched with the wear of working hard and laughing hard. Tactile and open as they were, I felt that I was among family as soon as I had crossed the Yugoslav frontier. From that moment, I recognized that I was not only in another country, but another world as well, one that had been stitched together into a brilliant patchwork quilt of languages, lifestyles, and customs. Between Trieste and Krk I heard Italian, Slovenian, Croatian, and Macedonian, and I saw businessmen, gypsies, grandmothers, and soldiers, all riding the same trains, all busy about their lives. And I was part of that crowd.

The old man on the island of Krk walked with me a kilometer or so.

He had been to Chicago once, he told me in halting monosyllables. Then he stretched his arms wide, rolled his eyes, and pronounced, "America!" He continued to accompany me down the road, finally depositing me at a gravel walk which led to a white stucco cottage with a clay tile roof. And then, without warning, he gathered me in his arms, gave me a bear hug, and, before he left me, enunciated, "Chicago!"

I headed up the walk, through a front garden overgrown with brambles clutching an arbor long bereft of its grapes. But here and there blood-red roses, rambling now, poked through the thorny canes. I looked toward the doorway and saw an old woman, squat, kerchiefed, and with a long, gray, open sweater over her housedress. She stopped her sweeping and raised her moon face. Her eyes brightened, but with curiosity rather than recognition, for this visit was unannounced. When I reached her she released a barrage of Slavicisms—thick, consonant-laden chunks of language which fell upon me like a driving hailstorm. I mustered the few Serbo-Croatian words and phrases I had learned from a guidebook, but my pronunciation must have been indecipherable, for the old woman, my distant relative, only smiled benignly.

Salvation arrived in the form of an old man in tattered suitcoat embedded with soot. He came up the walk and joined us on the threshold, smiling toothlessly at me. Our conventicle hovered in awkward silence for some moments, when, on a whim, I addressed the man in German. He nodded and identified himself as a chimney sweep. I explained who I was, and he translated to the woman. She threw her broom down, embraced me, and began to wail, pushing me away and clutching me to herself by turns. She kept repeating a phrase, an exultation, which I later learned was, "The son of my daughter-in-law's cousin!" Soon the neighbors had arrived, along with their children, as the word had spread among them like a lit fuse: "The son of her daughter-in-law's cousin!" In the next moment roses were brimming in my arms and I was sitting in a small, cozy kitchen, eating dumplings.

Her name was Marija. She was seventy-nine. She lived alone in her cottage but was well looked after. Every few days a huddle of nuns came by with bread and other staples. The afternoons saw frequent visits from neighbors and from the children next door, Ivana and Katrina. Marija showed me family photos—sepia-toned images of people long since passed away. She fed me chicken and egg dishes and sat with clenched hands, watching while I ate and speaking to me in a language which was as impenetrable as lead shielding. I tried to help her, to lighten her work where I thought I could, but she would not allow it. One day I accompanied Marija to the woodshed. She limped along, lightly swatting her bad leg with a branch, repeating, *"Noga, noga, noga,"* in reference to the affected limb. But when I reached down to gather the wood for her, she swatted my hand away, shook her head, smiled, and carried the wood herself.

I stayed four days with Marija. After the second, I felt at home. By the third, I didn't want to leave. I was not only happy, but also incorrigibly curious as to who would enter the house that day and what their story would be. When I look back on that time I am filled with images and sensations which can only be appreciated when life is lived in slower motion: turnips simmering in a white enamel pot on a cookstove, a man replacing a clay tile in his roof, a child suspended in a hammock among raspberries and roses, three elderly nuns giggling like schoolgirls at the sight of a stranger, a churchbell ringing in the evening, an elderly couple tending their flower boxes . . .

On the fifth day, I left. Marija gave vent to her emotions, her weeping punctuated by the clip of her shears as she gathered roses from in front of her house. She thrust them into my arms, embraced me, released me, embraced me again. The leave-taking was almost unbearable, but I showed no resistance to her sentiments, because in Marija's eyes I deserved nothing less, for I was the son of her daughter-in-law's cousin.

A Culinary Wish Comes True, Briefly

I've always been willing to clean up my own dirt, do my own wash, and mend my own clothes. But if I had the financial wherewithal, I'd hire a cook. Before I adopted my first son, I subsisted on minimalist meals: beans and franks, macaroni and cheese, BLTs. My disdain for cooking was such that I wanted to get in and out of the kitchen as quickly as possible, so as not to have to spend too much time doing the thing I do least well.

It's not that I can't cook; it's just that I have no instinct for it. I can't remember recipes, and I have absolutely no capacity for innovation: if a recipe calls for oregano and all I have is "Italian seasoning," I'll abandon the project and escape to McDonald's. This lack of "feel" for the art of cooking has always made it a joyless act for me.

But when my son Alyosha arrived I knew, of course, that I would have to mend my ways. I needed to start thinking in terms of balanced meals, of fruit versus Suzy Q's for dessert, and of enough variety to entice him to sit down at the table with something resembling anticipation.

I think I've failed at this, too. When I prepare meals for my son, it's like presenting a prince with an exotic dish from a newly discovered land. He sits there, staring straight ahead, while I hover over him with cautious optimism, bearing a covered casserole. I set it down in front of him, remove the lid, and watch for his reaction. On rare occasions he firms his lip, nods, and quietly accepts the repast as I sigh with relief. Normally, though, he hangs his head and massages his nine-year-old temples. "How sad," he seems to be saying. "How sad."

I recently shared this woe of mine with a friend who has a knack for coming up with tasty, satisfying, healthy meals in an almost incidental manner, while carrying on a phone conversation and holding a two-year-old in her arms. She plainly has a culinary gift. As I sat at her table, watching her cook, complaining bitterly about my morass, she asked, "What would you do if you had one wish?"

My eyes glazed over as I stared into the distance. I described the ideal situation. "If I had the money," I told her, "I'd hire a woman from Bolivia. She'd be grandmotherly, round, draped in a serape of many colors. Her name would be Pascuala. While I was at work and my son in school she'd be at my house cooking. And when we returned home at the end of the day, there would be a hot South American meal steaming on the table. We'd sit and eat, with Pascuala standing over us, wringing her hands and crying tears of joy. At the end of the meal my son would leap into her arms, cover her with kisses, and say 'Thank you' a thousand times."

My friend shook her head and firmed her lip, as if to say, "How sad."

A propitious moment arrived when my son returned home from school one day and told me his third-grade class was studying the rain forest.

Inspiration struck. Why not, I proposed, go to visit a rain forest? I checked with the travel agent and found that tickets were more than reasonable. As a final touch, I used my computer to hunt up a Costa Rican family willing to host us.

We were off. Not only did a promising trip lie ahead, but I wouldn't have to cook for ten days.

Costa Rica was as breathless as I had heard. It has two beautiful coasts, extensive rain forest, and a generous, open people. The family we stayed with had forty members—though not under one roof. Alyosha and I lived with the matriarch. She and her sons and daughters and grandchildren treated us like family, and we grew close and confiding in very quick time.

I took my son into the rain forest. We saw the requisite monkeys, parrots, and outsized insects. It was clear that this was what my son would remember about the trip. But what gratified me most was a daily event that was, indeed, a dream come true.

While Alyosha and I were out seeing the country, our hostess, the señora, who always rose at 4:00 A.M., was home cooking. When we returned in early evening, there, sitting on the table, were plates and bowls of beans, rice, chicken, mangoes, fresh bread, and seasoned tomatoes, aromatic to the point of making my cheeks ache. The steam seemed to rise up and twist itself into fingerlike wisps, beckoning us to sit and enjoy. We did sit, and we did enjoy, Alyosha no less than I. And the señora? She sat at the end of the table, her hands clasped, nodding with pleasure that we took such satisfaction in her cooking. The only thing lacking were her tears, but one can't have everything, especially in a strange country.

When we left this dear family, my son was saddened at parting from his newfound friends. As for me, I couldn't take my mind off the cooking. The señora wrote down some of her recipes for me, but, in my hands, they tasted no better than day-old hash once I tried to reproduce them back in Maine.

I think I'm a little better for the experience, though. At least I know what good food is supposed to taste like, and this inspires me to keep on trying. As for my son, he seems to have become more forgiving toward my efforts in the kitchen, realizing perhaps that, although I will never have my Pascuala, I really am doing my best. But, for ten days I had a taste of my dream, and, as with any ideal, even a taste is a gift that must be accepted with humility and gratitude.

A large part of raising a child is teaching him or her how to make appropriate choices in life. I have been generally proud of the choices my son Alyosha has made, but it wasn't until recently that I realized how much I sometimes benefit from them as well.

Alyosha is a robust, ever-busy fourteen-year-old who is fully invested in his middle school experience. This year, for the first time, he is studying French, a language of which I have no command and a culture for which I feel no particular affinity.

As a result, I have stayed largely aloof from my son's foreign language homework, happy that he seemed able to manage it on his own. One night, however, out of curiosity, I interrupted him to ask how his French was going. He put down his pencil and looked up at me. "Dad," he said, biting his lip, "I really want to go to Paris."

"Paris?" I echoed, in an attempt to buy some time to take his answer in. And then, "Are you kidding?"

In my own defense, I need to add that when this conversation occurred we were in deepest winter in Maine, with the wind howling about the eaves and snowdrifts all but barring entry to the front door. The very thought of leaving our warm and cozy home, much less flying out over the North Atlantic, was absolutely unappealing. But still, I felt a need to give his idea due consideration. "Paris," I said again, rolling the word around in my mouth like a hard candy. "Why Paris?"

To make a long story short, Alyosha's French teacher, or the language, or perhaps a combination of both, had inspired him. "I really want to go," he begged. "There's something about it." Then, having planted the thought, he returned to his vocabulary list.

I spent the next several days ruminating on the subject. I had never been to Paris, but I had to admit I harbored some subtle biases about the French, especially the Parisians, whom I understood to be, in a word, difficult, especially about Americans who couldn't stitch the simplest French phrase together. Well, that was me to a T, and the prospect of scurrying about and begging for directions in English on the Champs-Elysées was not a heartening one. I did have a little money set aside, but I had intended it for a computer that we could both use.

About a week later I approached my son at his homework once again. "Alyosha," I nudged. "About Paris . . ."

His head bobbed up and he smiled at me. "Yes, Dad?"

"Well, we do have a little money, but we have to make a choice. I wanted to get a computer, which will be even more important once you start high school next year. But we can't afford both a computer and a trip to Europe right now."

"Does that mean . . . ?"

"You'll have to choose."

My son has a capacity for action that is exceeded only by my gift for procrastination. He looked dead at me and fired one word—"Paris."

I couldn't believe he had opted for travel over a computer. Over Space Invaders! Nascar! Instant Messenger! But I felt there was no going back. Had I given him my word? I guess I had.

And so, late one January night, after Alyosha was fast asleep, I sat down at our outdated computer and did my homework, waiting for Web information to drip onto my screen like slow molasses. After three hours I had done it, for better or worse. I had bought two cheap tickets to Paris and booked an inexpensive hotel room in the Latin Quarter, wherever that was.

During the ensuing weeks Alyosha's anticipation grew, and he was the center of a great deal of attention in his French class. Even his teacher was wringing her hands with vicarious joy. To tell the truth, my enthusiasm was growing as well, especially as I pawed my way through my copy of *Let's Go France* and discovered that Paris would be significantly warmer than Maine.

In the middle of February we commenced our trip on the tail end of a heavy snowfall. We headed north, out of Boston, out of snow country, and, six hours later, into a place that had until that moment been little more than an abstraction for us.

From the moment we landed in Paris, Alyosha went on autopilot. He had seemingly flash-memorized a map of the somewhat oval-shaped city, enumerating all the sights and the best ways to get to them. On the first day, after we had settled into the hotel, we stepped outside and my son immediately took me by the coat sleeve. "Let's see Notre Dame first!" he gushed as I scrutinized my folding map. "Now wait," I counseled, ever the voice of caution and moderation. "It says here . . ."

"Follow me!" sang Alyosha, and it was all I could do to stay within earshot as he ran off down a narrow street permeated with the aroma of fresh baguettes.

And so it went. The Louvre, the Eiffel Tower, Versailles. Tiny Greek restaurants and French cafés. Long walks through ancient, winding streets and, on our last evening, a boat ride down the Seine with all of

Paris illuminated before us. As we sailed past the Eiffel Tower, the clock struck nine and its latticework exploded with thousands of flashing lights.

My son looked at me and I could see two miniature, sparkling Eiffels reflected in his eyes. I sensed that he wanted to tell me something, but I felt compelled to speak first. "Good choice, Alyosha," was all I managed. "Good choice."

ONE SMALL DIVE, ONE GIANT LEAP TOGETHER

When my son Alyosha appeared in my life, I promised myself that I would give him experiences which would burnish his spirit and broaden his horizons. A scuba adventure was one of these. I have been diving for over twenty years, and ever since my inaugural dive in the cold, clear waters of New England, I had envisioned taking a child of mine under the sea.

Events finally aligned themselves in our favor only a few weeks back. A colleague of mine was house-sitting in the Dominican Republic and invited us down for a visit. I was unsure about being able to accept her offer until, one day, a line of e-mail illuminated my computer screen: "The diving's great."

Before Alyosha could fully get his mind around the idea of the Caribbean in the off-season, we were winging our way south to a place as different from Maine as can be. From a land of pine woods, blueberry barrens, and a bitterly cold ocean, we soon arrived in a place of coconut palms, pineapple fields, and a sea of striking clarity and welcome warmth.

One day, while we were walking along a beach on the island's north coast, I spotted a dive shop, and opportunity beckoned. "Hey," I remarked to Alyosha as I gravitated toward the shop, "look at this."

My son was mildly curious and trailed along. We watched as the Dominican divemasters readied a batch of tourists for an underwater outing. Alyosha noticed that one of the customers was little older than he. My son looked up at me, and I arched my eyebrows. "How about it?" I queried. "The water's warm."

After a moment's hesitation, Alyosha assented. I explained to the divemaster that my son was a newcomer. "No problem," he said. "I'll show him everything he needs to know."

I watched as the man sat my son down and went over the equipment and safety procedures with him. "I'll be with you all the time," he reassured Alyosha. And then, glancing up at me, he added, "So will papa."

A short while later we were in a boat, motoring out at a good clip to the dive spot about a hundred yards offshore. It was a bluebird day: clear sky, brilliant sun, and cooperative sea. We anchored, and the tourists plopped into the water to a waiting divemaster, who took them, one by one, down to the bottom. Alyosha was already in the water and bobbing at the surface as I donned the last of my equipment. He looked handsome in his gear, in a way that only another diver can appreciate. I could perceive through his mask, however, the slightest hint of apprehension in his eyes.

Then, before I was even out of the boat, the divemaster grabbed hold of my son from the front and deflated his buoyancy vest. I watched with apprehension as Alyosha disappeared beneath the gentle waves.

Suddenly, my head was filled with all kinds of unpleasant images of Alyosha down there without me, panicking as he forgot some detail of his cursory training. I adjusted my mask, bit into my regulator, and flopped over the side. Then I began my descent to the bottom, wondering if Alyosha would ever be able to forgive me for getting separated from him. I had wanted to give him a new experience, and now I was faced with the likelihood of having ruined it for him.

I continued my descent through the impossibly clear, blue water, making minor adjustments in my gear as the pressure increased. A few seconds later I felt bottom. I folded my knees and looked around for my son. Where on earth—or under the sea—was he?

And then I saw him, about five yards to my left, sitting on the bottom as placid as a pumpkin. I swam over to him, solicited his attention with the "okay" sign, and was rewarded with the broadest smile one can manage through a mask and regulator.

I reached out and took Alyosha's hand in mine. Lifting off from the bottom, slowly, we started on our odyssey, rounding one small reef after another. Here we saw a sea urchin reminiscent of a snowball with spines; over there was the long figure of a trumpetfish standing on its nose among some finger corals to give the slip to potential predators; and all about and between us swam the curious: fishes in shocking golds, blues, and reds.

We stayed under for thirty minutes, after which, our hands on each other's shoulders, we made our languid, angel-like ascent. We broke the surface and felt the warm Caribbean breeze wash over our heads. "How was it?" I asked Alyosha.

His reply was immediate. "Cool!" he exclaimed. "Let's do it again."

We did do it again. Only this time Alyosha took *me* by the hand and showed *me* the reef. Not a word could pass between us during those dives, but despite the silence, I can't remember when I have ever felt closer to my son.

THE TRAIN TO BERLIN

The train journey from Warsaw to Berlin seems interminable—a slow crawl made uncomfortable by frequent stops, delays, and a passenger load that causes the cars to list precariously at times.

Finding a place to sit is a task in itself, requiring both brawn and perseverance. But with my full backpack and Wolverine hiking boots, I was fit for travel, and travel I did, from one end of the train to the other, back and forth, again and again, uttering "*Przepraszam*" to squat, round-faced Polish grandmothers, and "*Verzeihung!*" to the stoic, forebearing Germans as my pack and I squeezed through crowded passageways in search of a compartment with a free seat.

It was late evening. The train was dark, except for an occasional waxen lamp. The air was filled with the viscous palatalizations of the Poles, underlain with the guttural enunciations of the Germans, the two tongues playing off each other in counterpoint. Facial features and language aside, I could still recognize a compartment of Poles—its six seats were occupied by at least eight, and food and drink were on ample display. I decided that the space could hold nine.

"*Przepraszam*—excuse me. Could I squeeze in?"

The Polish men half waved at me and then slid the glass door shut behind me. Their murmurs might have signified disapproval. I don't know. I wedged myself snugly between two who were asleep. I looked at the others and smiled. My gesture received only nods from haggard, unshaven, silent faces.

This essay was written when Germany was still a divided country.

I looked out the window at Pomerania—an eternal plain of black velvet littered with pearls. As my eyes adjusted to the darkness, details of my immediate surroundings gradually made themselves known. Several overstuffed bags and packages cluttered the area around each man—about his feet, in his lap, and in the overhead luggage rack. Guest workers. On their way to West Germany. And yet they filled the air with palpable trepidation. I didn't understand why. The West was opportunity and freedom. And light.

We had been twelve hours under way when we pulled into East Berlin. Every Pole in the compartment sprang to life as German shepherds were brought on board, mirrors were inserted under the train, and uniformed officials probed behind our seats with slips of wire. We all watched as the corridor pulsed and swarmed with life in transit. Many passengers had to get off in East Berlin: they had no authorization to proceed beyond the wall.

The Poles in the compartment looked frightened, and when another East German official burst in, they fumbled for their documents of passage, anxious to show that their situations were legal. They displayed their papers with the alacrity of fathers proffering photos of their children. "*In Ordnung,*" pronounced the German. But there were no smiles.

The Poles eased back into their places, and I listened for all of us as they breathed laboriously, making the air hot. And was it the throbbing of the locomotive revving up, or human heartbeats which fell against my eardrums like the surging of my own blood?

And then, the train seemed to lift itself, like a bubble floating to the surface of a lake—up, up, rising above the Berlin Wall, slowly, tenaciously. This was not a decision to be taken lightly. The East only grudgingly let her children go. The Poles pressed their faces to the window and looked down as the train moved out from dim, silent shadows to the defiant glare of the West. It was like sliding into home plate—in slow motion.

But I knew we were there when one of the Poles opened the window, wide, allowing the wind to blow in unrestrainedly. Then, his face suddenly aglow, he spread his arms and sang out in heavily accented German: "*Guten Morgen, Deutschland.*"

In contrast to the celebration that accompanied the demolition of the Berlin Wall in 1989, the fortieth anniversary of its 1961 construction passed almost unnoticed. If I hadn't seen a small blurb about it in the world news section of my local paper, I don't think I would have remembered it myself.

This, despite my having an actual piece of the wall mounted neatly alongside a photograph I took back in 1985, when the most formidable and durable structure created by East Germany still stood as the quintessential icon of the Cold War.

I have three distinctive memories of my interaction with the wall, each, in its way, denoting a certain poignant aspect of its existence.

I first saw—and touched—the wall during a Fulbright year in what was then called West Germany in 1984–1985. I was not living in Berlin, but knew that the erstwhile capital of the formerly united Germany would sooner or later be on my itinerary. Suddenly, in March, I was there, running my hand along the wall, over the myriad graffiti covering its western face, and then mounting an observation platform to view the bleak, heavily mined "no-man's-land" that formed a deadly buffer between the inhabited sections of East Berlin and the wall itself.

The very next day I decided to cross over through the notorious "Checkpoint Charlie." Sticking to the narrow, white-painted, prescribed path, I sauntered along to a window, where I obtained my day visa from the East German authorities before continuing on my way. A moment later, as I followed the path, a German motorist called to me from the auto route a short distance away. He had broken down and was beckoning for me to help him push his vehicle. Without thinking, I stepped off the path and began to walk over to him. Within the instant three guards were upon me, demanding to know what I was doing. With my hands up I explained—breathlessly—about the car that had gone kaput. The guards conferred. Then one of them grudgingly allowed me to go and offer assistance while he warily supervised my efforts.

My second interaction with the wall came a few days later. I was on a tour bus to East Berlin with other American Fulbrighters and their families. We alighted in the heart of the city and visited some approved sights, none of which I remember. But I did take note of a little boy of about eight in our tour group. He had struck up a friendship with a similarly aged East German boy who had gravitated over to the Americans. For the rest of the afternoon the two boys romped and laughed, each chattering in his own language. The time finally came to reboard the bus. As we headed for the checkpoint, the American lad hovered at the back window, waving and gesturing to his newfound friend, who was running to keep up with the bus. When we stopped at the checkpoint the two boys took advantage of the brief pause to shout to each other through the glass. And then the bus surged ahead. The East German boy tried to run after us again, but suddenly stopped dead in his tracks and stood there with his arms at his sides, staring long and hard as our bus slipped through the checkpoint. Then he offered a plaintive wave, took to his heels, and disappeared down a dark alleyway of his gray city.

The third and last time I saw the wall was in 1990 when it was being demolished. There were Germans and foreign tourists everywhere, hammering away, getting their own little chunks of history. I walked over to a place which only months before had been part of the no-man's-land—heavily mined, barb-wired, guarded. Now a Madonna concert was planned for that very spot. How surreal. One day a place of death, the next—music.

I didn't dwell upon these thoughts for long, for I had my hammer too. I approached an East German policeman who was standing, smiling and unarmed, by a section of the wall, where not long ago he would have been a dour-faced sentinel carrying a submachine gun. Showing him my hammer, I asked, "May I?" His smile broadened. "Help yourself," he said, "and have a good day."

And so I hammered away, feeling the weight of history in my hands. As I pounded the concrete, I didn't think of the wall as such, or of the Madonna concert, or that little Trabant I had helped push, or of decades of East-West tension. Rather, I imagined myself hammering a hole big enough for a boy to run through.

My ten-year-old son thinks I'm obsessed.

If I am the only parent who still corrects his child's English, then perhaps he's right—to him I would be an oddity, a father making remarks about something which no longer seems to merit comment.

I think I got serious about this only recently, when I ran into one of my former students, fresh from two months in Europe. "How was it?" I asked her, full of anticipation for her report.

She nodded three or four times, searched the heavens for the right words, and then informed me, "It was, like, whoa."

And that was it. The glory of Greece and the grandeur of Rome summed up in a nonstatement. My student's whoa was exceeded only by my head-shaking woe.

Perhaps as a biology teacher I shouldn't be overly concerned with my students' English. After all, the traditional refuge of the science instructor is the hated multiple-choice exam, where students are asked to recognize, but not actually use, language. English instructors are, however, duty-bound to extract essays and compositions and position papers from their charges. These products, I am told, are becoming increasingly awful. I still harbor the image of an English-teacher colleague who burst into my office one day in a sweat of panic. "Quick!" she commanded. "A dictionary!"

I watched as she tore through the book. "Just as I thought!" she exclaimed, pinning the entry with her finger. "It *is* spelled r-e-c-*e-i*-v-e."

Her point, whether she knew it or not, was that students make the same mistakes over and over again. As for their teachers, they must read hundreds and eventually thousands of repeat errors, which in time become more familiar than the accepted forms, so that the instructors themselves become uncertain whether it's rec*ie*ve or rec*ei*ve, prot*ie*n or prot*ei*n.

The one thing that stories about the demise of English in America have in common is that they're all true. And students usually bear the brunt of the infamy, because there is a sense that they should know better. The truth is that they are being mislead everywhere they look and listen. Supermarket aisles point them to the "stationary," even though the pads and notebooks are not nailed down; people "could care less," even when they couldn't; and, more and more, friends and loved ones announce that they've just "ate" when, in fact, they've eaten.

Blame must be laid (and lie, not lay, it does) somewhere, and I am happy to volunteer to place it squarely on the schools, which should be safe harbors for the standards of the English language. Instead, it's a rare one that teaches grammar at all. Or syntax or vocabulary. In fact, the younger teachers themselves have little knowledge of these underpinnings of the language, because they also went without exposure to it.

Without grammatical rules of the road to fall back on, students are dependent upon parroting the language they see and hear around them. Further, it makes formal transmission of the English language extremely difficult, and the acquisition of foreign language all but impossible: once a student is confronted with verbs and nouns, let alone the pluperfect tense, the inclination is to give up. Or, at best, to learn a pidginized version of a foreign tongue: "*Yo* Tarzan, *tu* Jane."

The schools having affirmed poor or sloppy speech habits through their lack of attention to them, I am obligated to do the dirty work of gently ushering my son Alyosha onto the path of competent communication. But, as the Wicked Witch of the West said in one of her rhetorical musings, "These things must be handled delicately." (Alyosha's patience is limited when his dad behaves like a teacher.)

The other day the two of us were driving to a neighboring town. As we set out on our five-mile trip, he noticed a bird in eccentric flight and said, "It's flying so raggedly." Impressed with his description, I remarked, "Good adverb."

Alyosha asked me what an adverb was. I explained that it's a word that tells you something about a verb. Which led to his asking me what a verb is. I explained that it's an action word, giving him the example, "*Dad drives the truck.*" "*Drives* is the verb," I told him, "because it's the thing Dad is doing."

Alyosha became intrigued with the idea of action words. So we listed a few more. *Fly. Swim. Dive. Run.* And then, having fallen prey to his own curiosity, he asked me if other words had names. This led to a discussion of nouns, adjectives, and articles. The upshot of all this is that within the span of a ten-minute drive, Alyosha had learned—from scratch—to recognize the major parts of speech in a sentence.

It was painless and fun, but it's not being taught in the schools. There seems to be a sense that as long as a student is making himself understood, all is well. Sort of like driving a junker that blows smoke and has a flat tire: if it gets you there, what's the problem?

Perhaps, then, language should be looked upon as a possession: keeping it clean and in repair shows concern and effort. It demonstrates attentiveness to detail and the accomplishment of a goal—clear, accurate, descriptive speech.

Just this morning Alyosha and I were eating breakfast together when I attempted to add milk to my tea. "Dad," he cautioned, "if I were you I wouldn't do that. It's sour."

"Alyosha," I said, swelling with pride, "that's a grammatically perfect sentence. You used 'were' instead of 'was.'"

"I know, I know," he said with a degree of weary irritation. "It's the subjunctive mood."

I was, like, whoa.

MY SECRET MOMENT IN THE POETRY SPOTLIGHT

I could hardly believe it. A flier. For a poetry recital. In this day and age. And it came out of my twelve-year-old son's school backpack, of all places.

Should I have been so surprised at this? After all, poetry is good stuff. In my own life I have made it a practice that every other book I read be a book of poems. And yet, I feel vaguely alone in this predilection for verse. The juggernaut of technology and science having appropriated elementary and high school curricula, not to mention that of colleges and universities, the humanities—especially the *ur*-humanity of poetry— seem to have been put up attic and are spoken of in whispers, like a discredited relative.

Ah, poetry, where has it gone? I can still see Mrs. Gooth of third-grade fame, standing before our class, swiping her broad arm like a maestro, conducting all forty of us eight- and nine- year-olds through the steady, rhymed cadences of such traditional gems as "I Wandered Lonely as a Cloud," "The Road Not Taken," and "The Tiger."

Like most of my classmates, I was willing enough to repeat the verses so long as I was sitting in ranks, chirping along with the rest. But I recall the sweat pooling in my palms when Mrs. Gooth began to scan the room for someone to stand before the class and recite solo. I was afraid that she had somehow discovered—through the clandestine methods available to third-grade teachers—that I knew the first stanza of "Sea Fever" by John Masefield. I loved that poem, with its resignations in shades of gray to yield to the pull of the ocean life. But I didn't love it enough to face my classmates and recite it.

My heart took flight when Mrs. Gooth's gaze passed over me and settled on Kevin Butler, who, to my amazement, marched right up to the front of the room and belted out "The Village Blacksmith" with the heart and fervor of an actor.

It has long been my theory that in America, interest in poetry declined in tandem with the rise of television. After all, school had once been the only show in town, with poetry one of its main acts. But the glitz and glare and incessant blare of the tube managed to make poetry seem old-fashioned. Print on the page was out; the vacuum tube was in.

The poem assigned to my son Alyosha was "In Flanders Fields." When I heard this I could barely contain myself. I immediately began to recite, "In Flanders Fields, the poppies blow / Between the crosses, row on row . . ."

"Dad," my son interrupted with a sad shake of his head. "It's my poem."

Oh.

As I watched Alyosha retire to his room, poem in hand, I felt driven to call my own father to tell him the news. No sooner had I mentioned "In Flanders Fields," than he began, "In Flanders Fields, the poppies blow / Between the crosses, row on row . . ."

Yes, he had learned it too. Back in the thirties. And it had somehow stuck, erupting once more to the surface, in memory yet green, after all these years.

A week later I was en route to the recital with my son. My sense of anticipation was strong: this was the highlight of my week. As we drove along I stole a moment to look down at Alyosha, who was quietly mouthing the words to his poem. I listened intently, and when he made some small error, I tried to correct him, but he held up a hand. Yes, yes, this was his poem, and my job was to drive and keep my mouth shut.

The atmosphere in his classroom was electric that evening. The room was packed with sixth-graders, their parents, and mostly younger siblings. My son's teacher, Mr. Glueck, bid us welcome and told us the program would last about thirty minutes—for nineteen students! Well, so it was a fast-food version of poetry, but as John Masefield would no doubt have concurred, any port in a storm.

One after the other the children came front and center. What an eclectic bunch: some were cleaned and pressed to perfection, and others wore jeans and baggy shirts; some were in costume, like the little girl who recited Leonard Cohen's "Joan of Arc," and others brought props, like the boy who recited "All Things Bright and Beautiful" with pet rabbit in arm.

Some students recited their pieces without batting an eye. Others were dumbstruck and warranted rescuing by Mr. Glueck, who dutifully prompted them. One girl made an exaggerated series of sounds unrelated to her poem, and I couldn't discern whether she was laughing hysterically, sobbing bitterly, or if poetry, like everything else, had simply progressed.

Alyosha, in white shirt and black vest, managed "In Flanders Fields" with only one brief lapse of memory. My fear was that he would become flustered if he noticed me mouthing the words. But he successfully ran his three stanzas down and then returned to the snug harbor of his folding chair.

After eighteen students had done their poems, Mr. Glueck announced that the last student, unfortunately, could not make it. I ran my eyes down the program and my heart sank. That student was supposed to recite "Sea Fever." Still one of my favorites.

As the gathering broke up and headed for refreshments and congratulatory hugs, I did the thing I did because the feeling was so strong within me. Seizing Mr. Glueck by the arm, I leaned into his ear and recited:

> I must go down to the sea again, to the lonely sea and the sky,
> And all I ask is a tall ship and a star to steer her by,
> And the wheel's kick and the wind's song and the white sail's shaking,
> And a grey mist on the sea's face and a grey dawn breaking.

I would have recited it in front of the class, but Alyosha was right: "In Flanders Fields" was his poem, and this was his night.

OF PILFERING, PEARS, AND POETRY

When I came to work the other day I was struck by an odor so sublimely sweet as to make my tastebuds ache. I followed the scent until it led me to the desk of the departmental secretary. There, lying on a paper towel, was a pear brimming with ripeness to the point that so much as touching it would have made the skin crack. The secretary herself was out of the office, and for a moment I actually contemplated seizing the fruit. Then she came in and temptation evaporated.

This was a coincidental circumstance. Just before coming to work I had been perusing a book of William Carlos Williams's poetry. Although I teach biology, I am constantly on the lookout for ways to marry literature to my discipline. This was the poem I had become stuck on:

This is just to say

I have eaten
the plums
that were in
the icebox

and which
you were probably
saving
for breakfast

Forgive me
they were delicious
so sweet
and so cold

There it was, then. This poem could just as easily have been written about Charlene's magnificent pear. It was as if Williams's poem had been illustrated in some wondrously olfactory way, and for the rest of the day I found myself preoccupied with a question which suddenly seemed dire: What has become of poetry?

During a recent lecture on the adaptations of plants and animals to their environments, I tried to tie in a poem by Robert Frost called "Design," in which he wonders at the purpose of nature's humblest inventions ("A snow-drop spider, a flower like a froth, / And dead wings carried like a paper kite"). The failure of some of my students to immediately catch the poet's meaning didn't faze me in the least, since that is the nature of poetry: one has to work at it. But what disturbed me was that about a third of those in the class had never heard of Frost. In fact, I was dumbstruck. For the longest time I brooded over the loss of poetry from our culture. How on earth could this have happened? If, in the words of Nobel laureate Isaac Bashevis Singer, "Literature is the memory of humanity," then we have become a nation of amnesiacs, especially when we forget the last of the great populist poets of America.

When I was in grammar school during the sixties, poetry seemed to be our constant companion from third grade on. It formed a kind of academic ether in which we moved. We simply took its presence for granted. The reverence with which Mrs. Gooth, my third-grade teacher, opened a book of poems indicated, in some subliminal way, that people who wrote stories were writers, but people who wrote poems were, well, Poets. And a Poet was a different kind of wordsmith altogether. Working from the environment within arm's reach, the ordinary and peripheral suddenly became unique and central. A red wheelbarrow, a crumpled newspaper in a snowdrift, a mouse . . . We were being fed the poetry of Williams, Frost, and Whitman without even knowing, in any intellectual sense, how these giants fit into the larger scheme of things.

But Mrs. Gooth's grave rendering of some of their lighter verses ("So—much—depends—upon—a—red—wheel—barrow," she would nod, her face laden with gravity) communicated the sentiment that these were words penned with the utmost care and therefore worthy of being remembered. And remember them we did—each student had to commit one poem to heart during the course of the school year. Joe Christiana, a noted bully on the playground, memorized the whole of Frost's "The Road Not Taken." This didn't make him any less a bully, but when he stood in front of his classmates and recited it, the cadence of the verse bore us away with him, and I felt myself compelled to acknowledge that there must be some good behind those fists.

In short, an exposure to poetry early on might not have made poets of many of us, but it did tell us that such things as poems existed—not a bad start for eight-year-olds.

Shortly after reading Williams's unassuming lines about the plums, originally written to his wife on a prescription pad, I came across my university's weekly newsletter, in which something called a "Poetry Slam" was being touted. As I understood it, this was the literary equivalent of tag team wrestling, in which aspiring poets, accompanied by visual and sonic effects, hurled themselves at a microphone in rapid succession and screamed their lyrics at the audience. Despite my love of verse, I didn't feel the slightest inclination to attend the event. Instead, a question cropped up in my mind: Why can't American poetry pull its own weight without the addition of bells, whistles, and acrobatics? In a sense, its development has paralleled that of the movie industry, where a film is valued not so much for its content as for its "special effects."

Perhaps one reason is that poetry is no longer taught in either our grammar or high schools in any uniform or consistent way, and therefore it has lost the "hallowed" quality these institutions could lend it. Now that it is being packaged to sell—with attached bangles, ribbons, and streamers—it has become just one more tawdry product of the age.

I think these ruminations eventually brought me to do the thing I did. When I returned to work the next day, the pear was still on Charlene's desk, doubly ripe now, begging for attention. Someone had left a note: "Charlene out sick." There it was, then. In another day the pear would be unfit for consumption, and so I took it, and in its place I left this note, as a sort of tribute to the unadorned act of poetry and to Mrs. Gooth's role in rooting it firmly in my life:

> *Charlene, This is Just to Say*
>
> *I have eaten*
> *the pear*
> *That was on*
> *your desk*
>
> *and which*
> *you were probably*
> *saving*
> *for lunch*
>
> *Forgive me*
> *It smelled so sweet*
> *and was about*
> *to go bad*

WHAT YOU SAID, AND WHAT YOU MEANT TO SAY

Quite a few years ago there was a much-reported incident reflecting Americans' ignorance of foreign languages. General Motors had marketed the Chevy Nova in Spain without thinking the ad campaign through. In the wake of miserable sales figures, it was finally pointed out that "*No va*" in Spanish means, literally, "It doesn't go."

I felt a singular connection to this story because ever since childhood I have been a foreign-language aficionado. When I was nine years old I spotted a paperback German-English dictionary in a pharmacy. I begged my mother to buy it for me. She did, and I immediately went home and began to write letters to Mr. Haller, the German TV repairman who lived on our street—by stringing together words from that dictionary, without regard for tense, syntax, or conjugation. I have no doubt now that the letters must have been largely indecipherable, which is probably why I never received any replies from the otherwise famously reliable Mr. Haller.

The moral lesson of that story is that it takes courage not so much to acquire a foreign tongue, but to go forth and put it to use. Inevitably, one has mishaps, and more often than not they are humorous.

Icelandic has been a linguistic pursuit of mine for years. I have made my share of atrocious errors in the language, but I have a good role model—a former Icelandic prime minister. Once, when he was at a formal dinner at the American embassy in Reykjavík, he was asked, after he had finished his meal, if he would like a second helping. Deliberating over the appropriate English response, he wanted to say what an Icelander would say, to wit: "I am so full I could burst." But he mistranslated the expression and came out with, "I am so happy I could spring."

And so it seemed only just that I, in turn, as an American of nondiplomatic rank, should commit my own faux pas in the very difficult Icelandic language. One day I was looking for the bus to a small location outside Reykjavík called Keldur. This place name in strict translation means "bog." When I asked the bus driver if he could "take me to Keldur," I used the wrong preposition and instead asked, with earnest intent, "Could you please put me in a bog?" In typically grave Icelandic fashion, the driver asserted that he could not, and I never reached my destination.

Another time I was driving through Iceland with some friends. After a long time in the car I wanted to ask if I could get out to "stretch my legs." Once again I fell victim to grammatical mayhem and instead asked, "Can we stop so I can tear myself limb from limb?"

The thing I have learned about foreign-language study over the years is that one must persist in spite of embarrassment, uncertainty, and discomfort. If one does not learn to bully one's way through a conversation, one will never learn to speak a language and will be forever relegated to the solitary and joyless task of poking through pocket dictionaries.

Of course, the spontaneous demands of conversation can also lead to the unexpected. During a recent trip to Ukraine to adopt my son, I was overjoyed at the judge's decision to approve my petition. When I returned to the orphanage I was still so emotionally lit that even my primitive Russian was deserting me. As the director of the orphanage hurried over to me I greeted her with *"Zdrastvuitye"*—a Russian version of "hello."

"I am so happy for you!" gushed the director.

"Zdrastvuitye!"

"You must be happy too."

"Zdrastvuitye!"

"You are doing a wonderful thing for this little boy."

"Zdrastvuitye!"

The thing is, I knew what I wanted to say, but I was hopelessly mired in a language ditch, my head elsewhere, my mental dictionary on hiatus. Why is it that now, in this moment of calm, the Russian words for "Thank you," "Yes, I am," and "It's nice of you to say that" are as apparent to me as my dislike of borscht?

I could, of course, tell story upon story about such mishaps: being on a German train and asking for "champagne" (*sekt*) instead of "mustard" (*senf*) for my bratwurst; telling a Russian acquaintance, upon entering her apartment in Moscow, that her home was very "red" (*krasny*) instead of very "beautiful" (*krasivui*); and informing a friend I was visiting on the coast of Spain that I intended to go out to "place" (*colocar*) shells on the beach instead of "collect" (*colectar*) them.

Now that an adoptive son from Ukraine has made his debut in my home, I am redoubling my efforts to improve my Russian. Of course, at the same time he will be developing his English. I wonder what will happen when our trajectories cross?

As always, my linguistic seatbelt is fastened.

It's everywhere one looks (and listens). "I *sunk* the boat." "I *shrunk* the sweater." "I *sung* the song."

What's a stickler for correct English to do?

The assault upon the past tense is one of several battles being waged on the linguistic war front. The "lay/lie" conflict has claimed many casualties, and even journalists have fallen before its terrible swift sword. I recently read, in a well-respected newspaper, that the subject of some disturbance was so affected that she "had to find a place to lay." I don't picture a victim seeking respite; rather, I envision a hen depositing an egg, surely not the image the reporter intended to convey.

Other conflagrations include the "further/farther" standoff, the "that/which" skirmish (hopeless, hopeless), and "between you and I," rapidly falling to the marauding enemy.

But the past tense! If all else be lost, this is where one can, and must, draw the line. If not, then all those elementary-school grammar drills, all those hours of repetitious toil, will have been for naught. It was Mrs. Gooth, my third-grade teacher—round as an apple and just as sweet—who introduced us to the formalities of English tenses. Did this not give her life meaning? Is it not her legacy?

There she stands, in memory yet green, ruler in hand, poised to conduct us eight-year-olds in our grammar drills like a choir. "For regular verbs," she pronounced in her hoity-toity voice, "the past is formed by adding -ed to the stem. However," she cautioned, "there are many, many verbs that do not follow this pattern."

By my count, there are precisely one hundred and eighty-seven. These so-called irregular verbs must be learned separately, so that "I swim" is not constructed as "I swimmed" (except in my six-year-old's lexicon) but rather as "I *swam*." And "I sink" is not "I sinked" but rather "I *sank*."

I sank. Sank, sank, sank. If I had my druthers I would charter a plane and drop this single word all over the country until, sunk (aha!) knee-deep in the leaflets, the masses would send up a collective cry of surrender as I flew (not "flied") happily home with a sweet smile of victory.

There are three principal parts of the verb: the base form, the simple past, and the past participle. Thus, "I stink, I stank, I have stunk." Why, then, do Americans insist upon rewriting this fixed grammar and reducing the forms to two—I *stink* and I *stunk*?

Perhaps this degradation has something to do with the American sense of economy, "downsizing" being one of the cultural themes du jour. All literate people are acquainted with the base form of "sing." I *sing* a song. But when it comes to the simple past, folks are increasingly, well, I wanted to say that they are increasingly stymied, but this isn't quite right. It's more as if they are unaware of the simple past, but instead make a beeline for the past participle ("I have sung"), give it a haircut, and then promote it to simple past as "I *sung*." This is a complicated maneuver. Wouldn't it be easier to simply retain "I sang" on its home turf, rather than go to the trouble of evicting it?

Apologists for the language will claim that English is a living entity, that it changes over time, and that the engine of that change is the vernacular of ordinary citizens. This is true, but only to a point. I would remind these "anything-goers" that, before its rules were written down, English changed so rapidly that it was indecipherable from one generation to the next. Such was the case with the *Peterborough Chronicle*, a yearly account of Anglo-Saxon life whose writing was suspended between 1131 and 1154. Within this span of only twenty-three years Old English had given way to Middle English, and folks could no longer comprehend the chronicle's earliest pages. I can think of no more compelling illustration of the need for fixed rules of grammar and exposition.

Ladies and gentlemen! The state of the language lies in the balance. Think of propriety, think of consistency, think of the generations to come. If these do not move you to action, think of Mrs. Gooth and her plaintive song of woe: "Sink, sank, sunk / shrink, shrank, shrunk / sing, sang, sung / stink, stank, stunk / ring, rang, rung . . ." This is the battle trench, the beachhead, the hardened bunker. If we do not achieve victory here, then what will be our fate when it comes to the more complicated forms of the past tense: drive/drove, forbid/forbade, slay/slew, and (gulp) forsake/forsook?

The enemy already has its answer, flourishing on the tongues of our children: Bring! Brang! Brung!

Whatever shall we do?

I recently made a personal resolution that had nothing to do with the new year. In fact, it's one I make from time to time and at which I repeatedly fail.

To put it plainly, I used to have beautiful handwriting. Every so often, evidence of past graphological glory surfaces: a sixth-grade essay on fire prevention; a fourth-grade theme (ah, whatever happened to the theme?) on a less-than-remarkable summer vacation; a book report on the Vikings . . .

What all of these treasures have in common is that they are appealing to the eye. My erstwhile celebration of perfectly symmetrical loops, swirls, and gently inclined letters has, over the years, degenerated into a jagged scrawl which I am able to overcome, to some extent, with only the most intense concentration.

Hence the resolution. This time it was initiated by the resurfacing, after all these years, of a certificate—an "Award of Merit"—for penmanship. Issued when I was in the seventh grade, it is reminiscent of nothing less than a college diploma, replete with gothic header and curlicues and signed by the members of the board of awards, C. O'Neill and M. E. Burke, their perfectly pedestrian names enmeshed in an arbor of calligraphical flourishes.

I don't think it immodest to say that I deserved that certificate. For it was the culmination of a process of handwriting development that began in the second grade (in the first grade we were not allowed to attempt cursive) under the tutelage of Mrs. Lempkin, a mere wisp of a woman with lusterless, jet-black hair who, brandishing her pen like a battle sword, led us headlong into the glorious ranks of what she ceremoniously called "The Good Handwriting Club."

Her standard was the Palmer Method, enshrined in a floppy booklet of exercises for the development of beautiful script. I can still recall with clarity the pages of loops, swirls, and broad zigzags, and eventually living letters, which danced from margin to margin, page after page, like ranks of infantry with one objective in mind: to vanquish the enemy called sloppy penmanship.

I grew to love those repetitive exercises, which Mrs. Lempkin approached as art. Especially the ellipses, drawn over and over again, the object being to develop a smoothness and continuity of hand, which, in due time, was applied directly, and with particular care, to the letters "O" and "Q."

In light of this background, I find it strange that penmanship is no longer taught in the grammar schools. How could something which was once considered so important suddenly be not spoken of at all? When I was in elementary school my assignments carried two grades, one for content and the other for handwriting. When, exactly, did the latter go by the wayside? I sometimes think that it is no coincidence that penmanship ceased to be taught in American schools upon Mrs. Lempkin's retirement.

I once broached this topic with a latter-day grammar school teacher. When I asked her if she valued good handwriting in her students she looked puzzled, as if I had addressed her in Albanian. After a moment's thought, she ventured the guarded response, "Well, they use computers nowadays."

It was clear that we were from different planets. In an age of increasing homogenization, when one can get the same food anywhere and strip malls are making all of our towns look alike, handwriting is as good as a fingerprint for establishing a beachhead on one's individuality. The signature is still evidence of uniqueness that even the courts stand by. The message of good handwriting: "This is you. This is your mark. Work at it, improve it, make it beautiful."

Which, of course, leads to another argument for truly good penmanship. Writing by hand is a relatively slow process—the slower the better, actually. The very physical act of slipping lines of wet ink onto paper is an almost organic connection between the writer and the word. And when one takes the time to emphasize shape, size and proportion, one is lingering with those words, giving them time to percolate down to the mind's centers of understanding, where they settle in for the long haul. Using a computer gets the job done, of course, but it is nothing like a spiritual act. It's more like doing the dishes.

So what is to be done about the current neglect? Mrs. Lempkin's solution was punitive. I can still see Michael McCrae, who had the worst handwriting in the school, standing at the blackboard, his hand quivering with exhaustion, as Mrs. Lempkin made him write, over and over again, "The Red Fox Jumped Over the Lazy Dog."

Perhaps it is the memory of that mortification that perches on my shoulder like a small, dark bird, admonishing me to take care, slow down, and remember the loops and swirls. I cannot deny that I use a computer for most of my writing these days, but for letters to friends and family I try to use a fountain pen and indelible ink, and I do my ut-

most to honor Messrs. O'Neill and Burke's estimation of my penmanship. In my mind's eye I envision my correspondents passing my letters
to friends and loved ones, perhaps over breakfast, and gushing, "What
beautiful handwriting!"

After all these years, I am still trying to do Mrs. Lempkin proud.

SPEECHLESS, BUT NOT FOR LONG

When I adopted my six-year-old son Anton he didn't speak a stick of
English. Isolated as he was in a small orphanage in a Ukrainian village,
I'm sure he wasn't even aware that there were languages other than his
native Russian.

Nevertheless, Anton was chatty almost from the beginning, and I
knew it would be interesting, to say the least, to observe the unfolding of
his English.

I had been through this before, with Alyosha. He was almost eight
when I got him. Within a couple of weeks he was uttering individual
English words (such as "No!"), followed by sentence fragments (such as
"I won't!"). Within several months he was speaking a pidginized English
("Me not want to!"). But then, one day, a perfectly constructed English
sentence, elegant and sophisticated, came out of nowhere. We were sitting at the kitchen table, eating pizza, a food Alyosha had not yet developed a taste for. After a few bites he pushed the plate away and declared,
"I will crave pizza no more."

His English had arrived.

Although Anton was younger when I adopted him, his English developed more slowly than Alyosha's. I attribute this to his being so much
more talkative than Alyosha was. Anton spoke so much Russian—often
to himself—during the first few months after his arrival that he self-
reinforced his mother tongue, making it harder for the English to penetrate.
But penetrate it has, with often comic—and sometimes exasperating—
results.

One of the first words Anton learned (and I fear it was from me) is
"disgusting." The problem with learning a new word as a child is that
one may get the pronunciation and general meaning right, but not the
context. The word exists in a sort of ether of misconception, sometimes

erupting inappropriately as it seeks its place in the wider waters of the language.

Thus it was that "disgusting" popped out of Anton with all the rat-a-tat-tat of a Gatling gun. I got him up one morning and handed him his socks. "That's disgusting!" he lamented. When I asked if he wanted to kick the soccer ball around he declared, "Disgusting!" with the same tone and inflection as if he were saying, "I'd love to!" The capper came one evening when we had friends over for supper. I brought the chicken dish to the table, and one of my guests remarked, "It looks delicious," to which Anton replied, "It's disgusting!"

Even when vocabulary develops to the point where real communication is possible, there are concepts which remain elusive. Time sense is one of these, as evidenced by this discussion about Christmas, which I had with Anton in July:

Anton: "When is Christmas?"

Dad: "Not for a long time."

Anton: "Tomorrow?"

Dad: "No, in five months."

Anton: "Is that the day after tomorrow?"

Dad: "No. Many, many tomorrows away."

Anton: "How many?"

Dad: "A lot."

Anton: "Three?"

Dad: "More than three."

Anton: "How many?"

Dad (doing a quick calculation): "One hundred and fifty-one."

Anton: "Tomorrows?"

Dad: "Yes."

Anton: "Is that today?"

Despite such mires, language acquisition is a thing to behold. There are those who assert that children simply parrot others until they have established a useful repertoire of words and phrases. But this is inaccurate, to say the least. I am convinced that Alyosha had never heard anyone say, "I will crave pizza no more." It was, so far as I know, an original utterance. In the same way, where on earth did Anton learn how to say, as he did not too long ago, "This toothpaste hates my lip"? Clearly, children do think about language and are very capable of creatively building the expressions they need from the language blocks available to them to get their meanings across (such as the fact that the toothpaste was irritating my son's chapped lip).

Anton completed kindergarten last June. He did well, but because of his English language deficit he had to act out many of his needs. Grabbing a crayon from another child was all he had to work with, since "Will you share that crayon with me?" was as unavailable to him as the equation for relativity. Likewise, a push substituted for "Please don't stand in my way," and an outbreak of tears conveyed the general message, "I wish I could say something!"

Now, at last, he can say something. In fact, he says many things, and he often says them incessantly, treating his new language like a toy he just can't get enough of. When he began first grade a couple of weeks back I hovered in the doorway of his classroom after dropping him off. I watched a clutch of boys chatting amiably about whatever it is six-year-olds talk about. And there, in the middle of the huddle, was my own boy, chewing his own share of the fat. And then, in a verbal gesture that might have been a shove only a few short months ago, he turned to one of the other boys and asked, "Would you share your crayons with me?" As it turned out, those words initiated a beautiful friendship.

For me, it is a singular pleasure that the precipitation of Anton's English in full came during the summer. Perhaps I owe something to this season for endowing Anton with a vocabulary of wonder as we swam, canoed, and explored the tangled riverbank behind our home. Just the other day we discovered a toad in the backyard. As I showed Anton how to hold and gently examine the creature he throbbed with excitement, finally coming out with, "It's so beautiful."

I didn't tell him that, compared to frogs, I had always found toads slightly, er, disgusting.

AN (ALMOST) UNSPEAKABLE LEGACY

I am the teacher turned student. I have given my last lecture for the day and now, with grammar and dictionary open on my lap, I am following the curves of the road which winds along the Penobscot River, en route to my Polish lesson. My third week, and already I am hopelessly behind, mired in a language so thick with consonants and diacritics that one needs a machete of a mind to admit a few rays of the light of understanding.

What inspired me to learn Polish well into my thirties I can't exactly say. I can remember as a child being hauled to relatives during the Christmas and Easter holidays. They would huddle in dense clusters in the tenement apartment of my great-grandparents, the white enamel stove seething in the background, bubbling with red cabbage and meaty pork stews. They spoke Polish, that indecipherable glue of a language, adhesive enough to yank the teeth right out of your head. (As once happened with my great-grandmother one Christmas Eve when I was five. She was rocking in her chair, nodding her kerchiefed head, when suddenly she began to call out for music. Violin music. "*Skrzypce! Skrzypce! Skrzypce!*" she spat, and her dentures flew—plop!—into her lap.)

"*Styczen, Luty, Marzec,*" I repeat to myself as I turn onto the approach road leading to my tutor's house. January, February, March. Part of my lesson for the week. Three decades have passed and done their slow work, erasing many of my family's babushkas and ham-fisted, baggy-pants men from the earth. And I am left mostly with sounds, trying to corral them with grammar, clothe them in cadence, so that my family has something more than the hasty "*Na Zdrowie!*" of a Christmas Eve toast and memories losing their details over time.

I pull into the driveway and fumble the books in my lap into a semi-neat stack, grateful once again for not having driven into the river while studying. I slip them into my briefcase and go up the walk to the front door. I knock. There is a rumbling of footsteps down wooden stairs. The door flies open. Her bleached hair is wild, for she never remembers exactly when I am coming. So she frantically primps and combs, waves me in, prompting me in Polish. "*Chodz! Chodz!*" she barks, but smiling, the sun skirting the tops of the pines on this October afternoon, passing through the kitchen window to strike her good side, giving her the demeanor of a kindly gypsy woman in the forest. She continues to speak Polish at me, rapidly, while clearing the table of books, papers, dishes. I smile and nod, repeatedly saying "*Tak!*"—the dumb affirmative of the ignorant. Then she looks up and gives me a flat smile. "Do you understand?" she asks. I hang my head. "*Nie,*" I admit. "Not really."

Her name is Jadwiga. She comes from a city in Poland called Bydgoszcz. Although she has corrected me a dozen times, I still pronounce it "By Gosh." I have known her for only three weeks, and already I have committed her life's story to heart. The escape in 1961 from Gomulka's repressive regime, her hiding in a freighter's coal bin with her two children as they sailed to France. "I was discovered!" she told me, shaking with terror even after all these years. But she had threatened the sailor with a fruit knife before stuffing his pockets with dollar bills as limp as old hankies. And so they survived.

After fifteen minutes of preamble—stories of her adventures and tribulations—the lesson begins in earnest. With eyes closed she claps her hands and stamps her foot, and I know by now what I am supposed to do. I begin to recite the first declension. The verb "to work." I am still very confused by it, but since Jadwiga is reciting along with me, I am able to bury my feeble response in hers. Until she stops and opens her eyes but continues clapping. Louder, faster, until I stumble and give silent thanks that my teeth are my own. "What's wrong?" she demands, rapping on the table. "You didn't study!" she concludes, scowling, no longer the kindly gypsy woman in the forest. Suddenly she has become the Beast of By Gosh.

"It is impossible," I despair, hanging my head. I kick the chair leg with my heel, feeling like a nine-year-old.

"The months!" she commands, spearing the air with her finger.

I rise to the occasion, reciting the months in order. In any language there is a certain helpful cadence to the months as each one prompts the next, like a rippling of dominoes. When I am done I look at Jadwiga. She smiles her gypsy smile and gets up from the table. When I do not know my lesson she hits me on the arm, harder than she knows. But when I have done well she gives me cake.

Sometimes I think I suffer too much for the legacy. If it were only nostalgia that drove me I would reject such a motive for learning Polish. "How is that possible?" I remember asking my father when he told me that my great-grandparents never learned English, although they had lived in America for sixty years.

My great-grandfather had worked for the New York Central Railroad, while my great-grandmother had stayed home as a seamstress. The train tracks formed the boundaries of their world: a low steel fence as limiting and threatening as razor wire and guard dogs. Hence all the relatives gathered at their tenement at Christmas, Easter, and Thanksgiving. Up the five flights of wooden stairs my parents would drag me, following the aromatic spoor of red cabbage and kielbasy, which competed with the smell of old blankets—the constant companion of the decaying tenements of the Jersey City waterfront of the early sixties.

A door opened, and there stood my kerchiefed great-grandmother, wringing her hands in anticipation, her face as round as the moon, her apron plastered with large, gaudy sunflowers. We, the world, had come to her, so why cross the tracks? Why learn English? I looked past her at my great-grandfather, who was struggling to rise from the sofa, where he sat next to the window which looked out over New York harbor, and in which the Statue of Liberty was framed.

I was eleven when the tenement was destroyed. The city struck it with a wrecking ball, scattering my relatives like bowling pins.

Jadwiga and I eat the cake. She rises and goes to the refrigerator. She opens the door, revealing a crystal pitcher of freshly made iced tea. It is chock full of ice, which chuggles as she lifts the pitcher and sets it on the table. The vessel is covered with daisies and sunflowers, and for a moment I think it is the most beautiful thing I have ever seen. I place my palm against its roundness and feel the cold.

Jadwiga begins to teach me a new declension. Amazingly, I seem to catch on quickly, using the partially learned first declension as a template. We run through it three times, together; then she says, "Now you." With great effort I begin to recite, moving my mouth in ways to which it is not accustomed. The singular goes well, but in the plural I falter. There is a form for addressing men, one for addressing women, and even one for addressing a thousand women if there is a man hiding among them. "It's hopeless!" I lament, but not with enough despondency that she will hit me. But neither will I get any cake.

Jadwiga slaps the table. Now she is going to encourage me, in her own way. She looks dead at me. I stare into her face and read her expression: *I am the one who stood in bread lines for hours on end; I breathed the coal dust of a freighter, surviving by the grace of God; I left the University of By Gosh to clean toilets in Portland's federal building. And you complain because Polish is hard?*

I swallow and go on, attempting the declension again. Slowly but surely I wring it out of myself. It is physically painful. Perhaps my great-grandparents weren't strong enough to learn another language. Perhaps they didn't learn English for fear of losing their hard-won Polish. Perhaps we are entitled to only one language at a time. You say you want French? Then trade in your Italian. Polish? Hand over your English first. The thought of being trapped in a no-man's-land between tongues alarms me. But for only a moment, for my reverie is broken as Jadwiga plops a pile of reading material in front of me. "The first story is about

Frederick Chopin," she says. Only his name reads *Fryderyk Szopen*. My mind refuses to juxtapose an *s* and a *z*. It brings back bad memories of "syzygy"—the word that bamboozled me in the eighth-grade spelling bee at Sacred Heart School. "What's wrong?" asks Jadwiga. "Why don't you read?"

I move my mouth, but no sound comes out. It is the syzygy effect, and I suddenly see Sister Mary Placid in the audience in 1968, mouthing the words: "I-am-so-disappointed-in-you."

Somehow the Rock of Gibraltar is lifted from my mind and I find myself reading, my tongue excavating *sz*'s, *dz*'s, and *zsyp*'s from some Old Slavonic quarry that had been given up for nonproductive. I can understand only one word in ten, but I do manage to pronounce them accurately enough that Jadwiga's face broadens into a bright smile. I gaze through the pitcher of iced tea. Its flowers drift out of focus and settle over Jadwiga, and this woman of By Gosh, I realize, is somebody's mother, somebody's grandmother, and, if she is as indestructible as the Polish women in my family, she will live to be a great-grandmother as well. Five minutes later I am in my car, and I think of my relatives, of hot red cabbage and painted eggs and the kick of the polka and Chopin's mazurkas and the poetry of Czeslaw Milosz as I drive home in the rain.

CREDITS

All of the essays in this collection first appeared in *The Christian Science Monitor* except for the following: "The Joys of Science," which appeared in *Newsweek;* "Martian Life? Ye of Too Much Faith," which appeared in the *Bangor Daily News;* "Clarinet Lesson" and "Joe Piranha Days," which appeared in *Buffalo Spree Magazine;* and "Shuffling toward Moscow," which first appeared in my book *Adopting Alyosha: A Single Man Finds a Son in Russia,* published by the University Press of Mississippi, and is reprinted here with the permission of the author and the publisher.

"Now Close the Windows" and excerpts from "The Ax-Helve," "Good-By and Keep Cold," "The Witch of Coös," and "Design" from *The Poetry of Robert Frost,* edited by Edward Connery Lathem. Copyright 1915, 1923, 1934, 1969 by Henry Holt and Company. Copyright 1936, 1951, 1962 by Robert Frost. Copyright 1964 by Lesley Frost Ballantine. Reprinted by permission of Henry Holt and Company, LLC.

Excerpt from "Personal Helicon" from *Opened Ground: Selected Poems 1966–1996* by Seamus Heaney, copyright 1998 by Seamus Heaney, reprinted by permission of Farrar, Straus and Giroux, LLC; and from *New Selected Poems 1966–1987* by Seamus Heaney, reprinted by permission of Faber and Faber Ltd.

Excerpt from "Axe Handles" from *Axe Handles* by Gary Snyder, copyright 2005 by Gary Snyder, reprinted by permission of Shoemaker & Hoard Publishers.

Robert Klose is a native of New Jersey but has been living in Maine since 1981. He teaches biology at University College of Bangor. He is the single father of two adoptive sons, from Russia and Ukraine, and a regular contributor of essays to *The Christian Science Monitor*. His work has also appeared in *Newsweek, The Boston Globe, Reader's Digest, Exquisite Corpse,* and elsewhere. He is a four-time winner of the Maine Press Association's annual award for opinion writing.